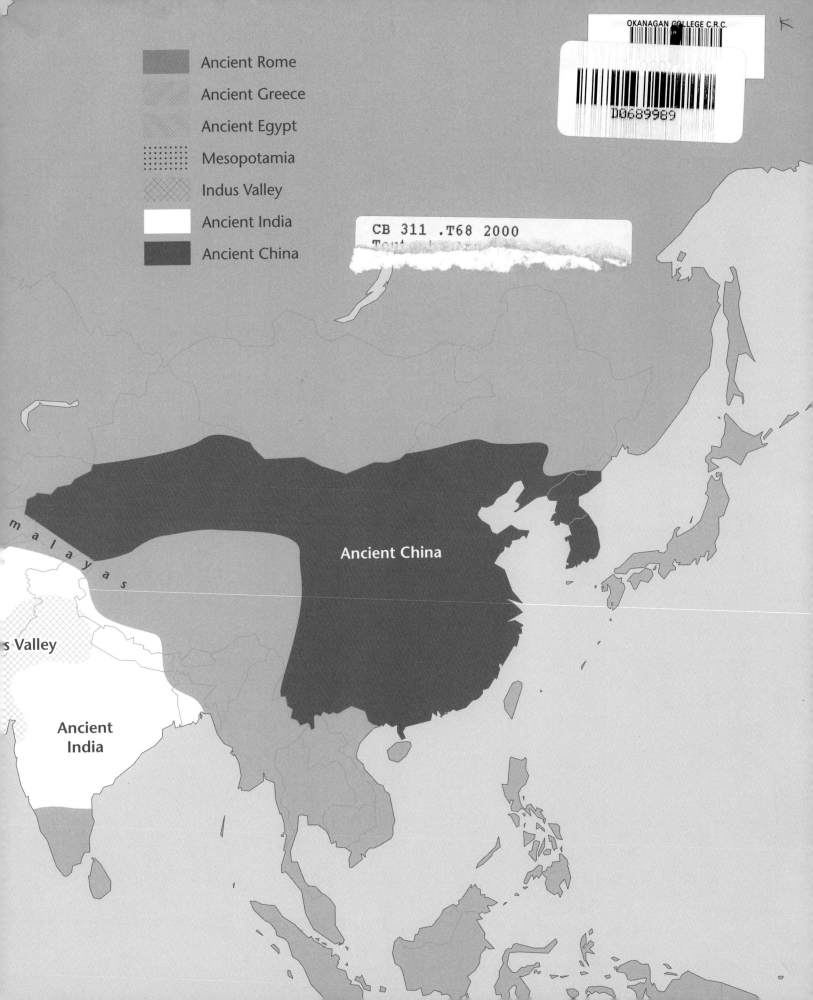

Ancient Rome

Ancient Greece

Ancient Egypt

Mesopotamia

Indus Valley

Ancient India

Ancient China

Ancient China

malayas

s Valley

Ancient
India

Ancient Worlds

OUTLOOKS **7**

ARNOLD
TOUTANT

SUSAN
DOYLE

OXFORD
UNIVERSITY PRESS

OXFORD
UNIVERSITY PRESS

70 Wynford Drive, Don Mills, Ontario M3C 1J9
www.oupcan.com

Oxford New York

Athens Auckland Bangkok Bogotá Buenos Aires Calcutta Cape Town
Chennai Dar es Salaam Delhi Florence Hong Kong Istanbul Karachi
Kuala Lumpur Madrid Melbourne Mexico City Mumbai Nairobi Paris
São Paulo Singapore Taipei Tokyo Toronto Warsaw

with associated companies in Berlin   Ibadan

Oxford is a trade mark of Oxford University Press
in the UK and in certain other countries.

Published in Canada
By Oxford University Press

Canadian Cataloguing in Publication Data

Toutant, Arnold, 1938 –
Ancient worlds
(Outlooks ; 7)
For use in grade 7.
Includes index.
ISBN 0-19-541435-7

1. Civilization, Ancient – Juvenile literature. I. Doyle, Susan, 1952 – . II. Title. III. Series.

CB331.T68 2000   930   C00-930791-5

5 6 7 – 03 02 01

This book is printed on permanent (acid-free) paper ∞.

Printed in Canada

Contents

Introduction

Ancient Worlds is a story about your past. Not your past alone, of course. It's also about the past of every other member of the human family throughout time. It tells how we find out about our origins in early times, how civilizations developed, and how the lives of people in those times are like and unlike our own.

The story you'll discover in Ancient Worlds is full of struggle and achievement, disaster and success, and certainty and speculation. As you read about ancient civilizations, you'll see that life on earth was once quite different. In many ways, though, life was just the same—our ancient ancestors faced many problems and choices similar to those we face today. Just like us, they sought answers about how best to survive on earth and how to improve their way of life.

The human story is still unfolding today. We are still searching for ways to make the world a better place. Think about the ideas in Ancient Worlds, especially those in the final chapter. You'll find suggestions for ways you can take action to improve the world around you.

As you learn about our long-gone ancestors, think about this: one day our civilization will become ancient history, too. What will the Grade 7s of the future think about the choices we make today? Perhaps your travels through this book will inspire you to make sure that we make good choices.

Chapter 1

Connections with the Past

In what ways are you connected to the past?

You have an **individual past**. This is the story of your life. All through your life, you will store up memories of your past—of the things you learn, the people you meet, and the special things that happen. You rely on this knowledge to make sense of new experiences.

Each of us also has a shared past as a member of the human race—we call this our **collective past**. This story of humankind begins when humans first walked the earth, and continues until a moment ago. Learning about our collective past helps us find out who we are as members of the human family.

The people who lived before us faced the daily challenge of meeting their basic needs. You will see that we face some of the same challenges today. In this chapter and throughout this book, you will learn more about our connections with the past.

Your Individual Past

Think about your own personal history. What events and experiences do you remember from your life? You probably remember the first time you tried a new skill, such as learning to ride a bicycle, or special occasions, such as your first ferry ride. But you probably don't remember many things that you know you must have done, like learning to walk or speaking your first words. You can find out about your personal past, and the past of those who care for you and raised you, by doing a little digging.

Finding Out About Your Personal Past

A student named Rebecca wanted to find out about her personal past. She began by asking questions—a lot of questions. "What did I enjoy doing when I was little? Where was I born? What else happened in the world on the day and during the year I was born? When did I take my first steps?" Then she drew a web to figure out where she would get her information.

Rebecca created a web to plan how she would gather evidence for her personal history. Think of another **source**, or place where Rebecca could get information.

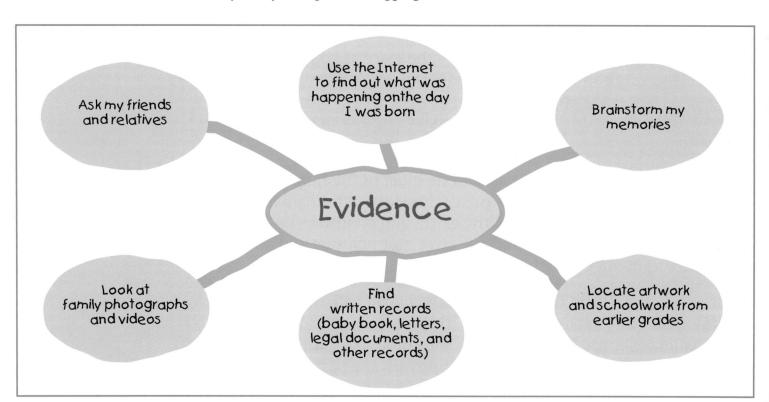

Ask my friends and relatives

Use the Internet to find out what was happening on the day I was born

Brainstorm my memories

Evidence

Look at family photographs and videos

Find written records (baby book, letters, legal documents, and other records)

Locate artwork and schoolwork from earlier grades

Rebecca and another student, Rabia, share items from their early lives and from the homeland of their parents. What do you learn about Rebecca and Rabia by examining this picture?

Rebecca collected the information and studied each piece of evidence. She made notes about what each piece told her. She asked herself if she'd answered her questions, or if she needed to go back and look for more information. After putting her information in order, she used it to write an **autobiography**, or story of her life. As she did so, she tried to keep in mind her chosen audience, her parents.

What steps did Rebecca take to gather information about her past?

 # Research

Whether you're looking for information about computers, the origin of the human species, or the menu of the local pizza outlet, it's all research. The order in which you do things may change. Sometimes you end up back at the beginning, but usually you follow the same steps. And you continue to ask questions in all steps of the process. Look over the steps on the next page to see which ones you have used in the past and which ones are new to you.

Research in Four Steps

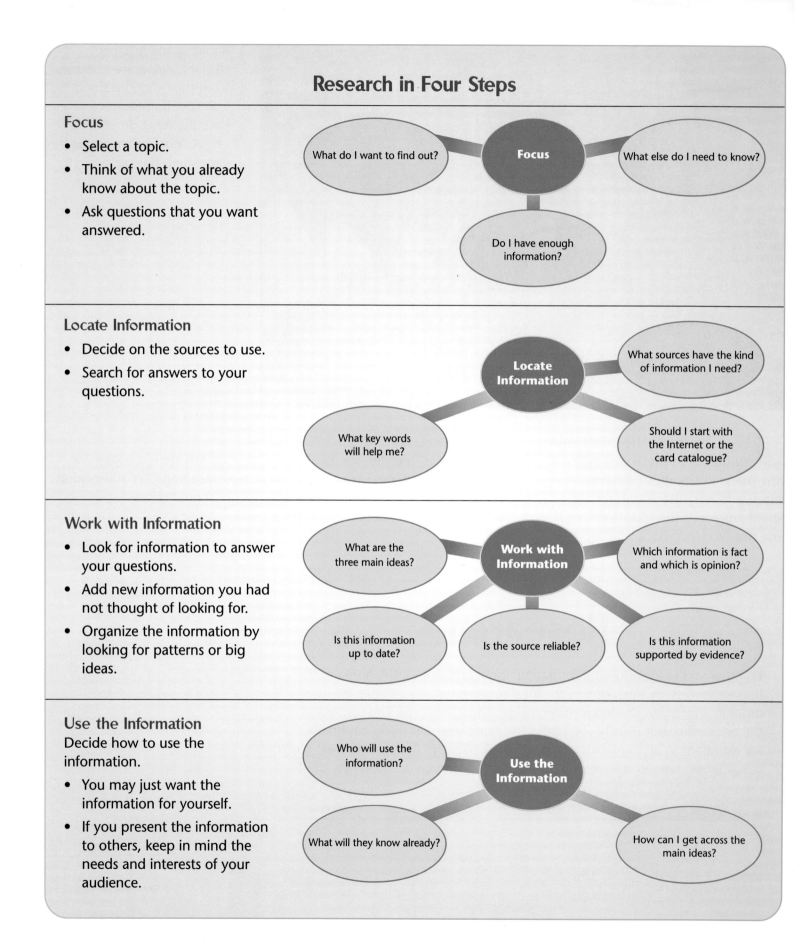

Focus

- Select a topic.
- Think of what you already know about the topic.
- Ask questions that you want answered.

Focus

- What do I want to find out?
- What else do I need to know?
- Do I have enough information?

Locate Information

- Decide on the sources to use.
- Search for answers to your questions.

Locate Information

- What sources have the kind of information I need?
- What key words will help me?
- Should I start with the Internet or the card catalogue?

Work with Information

- Look for information to answer your questions.
- Add new information you had not thought of looking for.
- Organize the information by looking for patterns or big ideas.

Work with Information

- What are the three main ideas?
- Which information is fact and which is opinion?
- Is this information up to date?
- Is the source reliable?
- Is this information supported by evidence?

Use the Information

Decide how to use the information.

- You may just want the information for yourself.
- If you present the information to others, keep in mind the needs and interests of your audience.

Use the Information

- Who will use the information?
- What will they know already?
- How can I get across the main ideas?

Investigate

Research to find out what the world was like on the day you were born. Begin by developing a web of questions such as the one below.

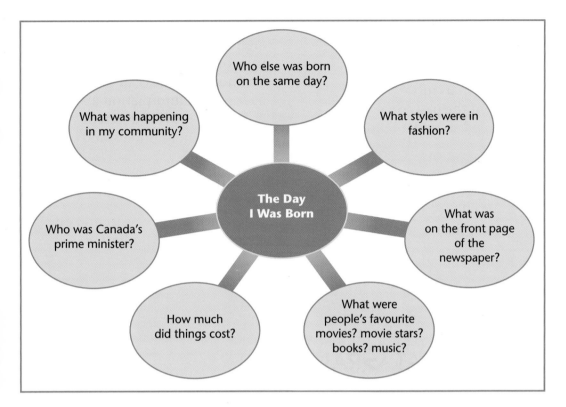

To organize your research, create a chart like the one below. Afterwards, decide how to share your work.

Your *topic*

The *questions* you asked

Your *sources* along with the *information* you found

A *summary*

Try www.famousbirthdays.com to see who else was born on your birthday.

Reading Hint

As you read, you'll come across words in heavy type, like "primary sources." Look for the definitions for these words in nearby text or in a sidebar or caption.

Historians usually use both primary and secondary sources when studying an event.

Finding Out About Ancestors

Finding out about what happened to us personally can give us only part of our individual past. We can learn more about who we are by finding out about relatives, ancestors, guardians, and other people connected to us in some way. To research the past, we use both primary and secondary sources.

Primary sources are written by people who take part in the event they're describing, or who saw the event taking place. Historians like to use primary sources to help them figure out what really happened. Primary sources can give a true view of the past, because the person writing the information actually saw what happened.

Secondary sources are written after an event has taken place by someone who was not there. Secondary sources can provide background information about an event, can provide different views, and can help us understand why things happen the way they do.

Read the following article to identify the kinds of sources that a girl named Leah used to find out about her great grandfather.

LEAH'S GREAT GRANDFATHER

One day in late 1998, Leah's grandmother told Leah that her great grandfather had died. Leah was surprised because she had never heard anyone talk about this relative. "I had a great grandfather?"

"You certainly did," replied her grandmother. "Sadly, though, I didn't know my father well—he moved far away when I was a small child."

Leah was curious about her great grandfather and wanted to know more about him. Her grandmother told her a few things. He had come from England as one of the "home children." These were children shipped to homes in Canada to work. Most of them were orphans. Between 1867 and 1939, about 100 000 home children came to Canada. Harry Knight, Leah's great grandfather, was one of them. Harry's mother had put her two sons into an orphanage because she had had tuberculosis and Harry's father had run off to seek adventure.

Leah asked her grandmother many questions. "When was my great grandfather born? When did he come to Canada? Where did he stay? What was his life like? Where did he live? What did he do for a living?"

"You ask so many good questions!" said Leah's grandmother. "I wish I could help you answer them all. Tell you what, I've got a box of his things. Perhaps that will give us some answers."

The two sifted through the box and discussed what each item told about Harry's life.

The birth certificate of Horace Aldolphus Knight shows he was born in Hampstead in the County of London, England. His birth date was February 9, 1908. His father was a bricklayer. Leah's grandmother said that Horace called himself Harry when he grew up.

A safety award received in 1949 suggests that Harry was a responsible person.

A copy of a book that Harry wrote, *The Well That Couldn't Be Tamed*, tells about Harry's life putting out oil-well fires in Alberta.

An old, undated newspaper clipping says Harry was born in Halifax, Nova Scotia, and that his father was a stonemason who was killed in World War One. Leah said that this was strange because the information does not agree with information on his birth certificate.

A small bundle of letters intrigued Leah greatly. They were letters that Harry had written to his mother while he was in an orphanage in Sussex, England, and then after he arrived in Canada. She noticed that the dates on the letters were mostly around Christmas and Harry's birthday. Harry wrote the letters, but he signed them from himself and his younger brother, Herbert. Leah also noticed that Harry repeatedly asked his mother to send him a photo of her so that he could remember what she looked like. Leah read through the letters and made some jot notes to make sense of them. Here you can see a few of them.

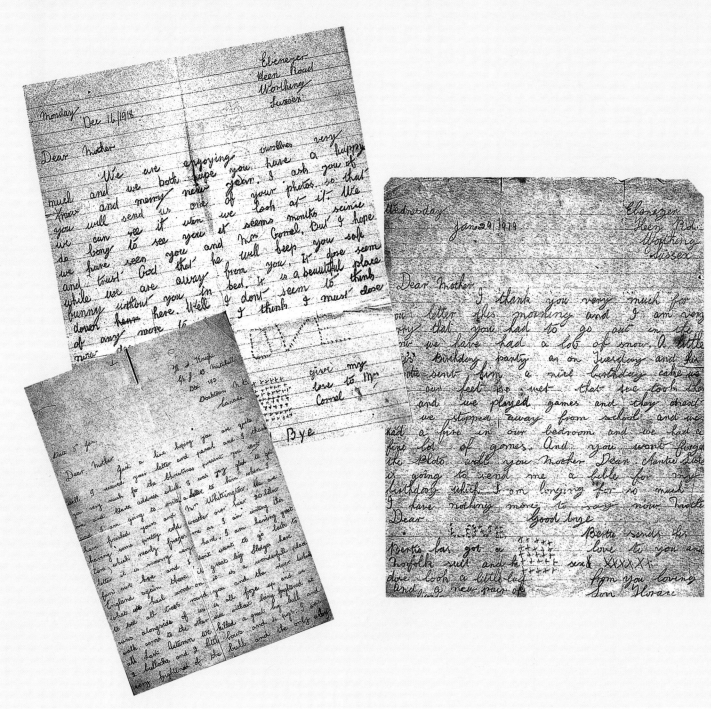

Great Grandfather at ten years old, December 17, 1918, in the orphanage in Sussex, England: "I ask you dear mother to send me one of your photos so that when we look at it we shall remember you."

At eleven years old, probably written in the winter of 1919, Box 183, New Brunswick, Canada: "I received your letter and money and photo which I was more than glad to get . . . . Times (are) very hard out here. There (are) people walking about starving to death. These people told me to tell you not to come."

At about twelve years old, 1920, no address. He thinks people want to kill him. Is that a fact or is he just upset?: "You know these people read my letters . . . They made me write . . . the other sheet and so I sneak to write this in bed to tell you to come to Canada. I have been fretting for you over three years and am so lonesome. Don't write any more so if you come they won't know . . . Don't . . . write whatever you do or else they will kill me. So come. Don't write."

At thirteen years old, no date, c/o James B. Mitchell, Doaktown, New Brunswick. My guess is that he wrote the letter in the spring because he talks about melting snow: "I have just heard that Mr. Mitchell has adopted me for his own son and they have made me tell you . . . . We have nice weather now, very warm and the snow is going. Times are very hard here and there is no work at all. I advise you to stay where you are and stick to your job."

Leah decided that she did not have enough information. It was difficult to piece everything together from the letters. To get a better picture of what life was like for home children, she did some research using the Internet and the library. To find out more about her great grandfather, she telephoned her great aunt in Toronto, who was Harry's half-sister.

Try This

Make a two-column chart to show how Leah gathered, recorded, and **interpreted** (made sense of) information. In the first column, list the points below. In the second column, state "Yes" if you think Leah did it or "No" if you think she did not. Be prepared to read evidence from the article to support your answers.

- Leah used both primary and secondary sources.

- She noticed when two sources disagreed.

- She gave reasons to explain her reasoning.

- She could tell the difference between fact and opinion.

- She did not make up her mind about things until she had evidence to support her views.

If you want to know more about **genealogy** (studying family history) check out these Web sites: http://www.cyndislist.com http://www.ogs.on.ca

Think For Yourself

Why do you think Leah wanted to find out more about her great grandfather? Is there someone you know personally who you would like to know more about? If so, write what you know about this person in a notebook or social studies journal. Explain why you want to know more.

Our Collective Past

All human beings on earth share one collective, or human, past. We share this past with people around the world today and also with people of ancient times. When we reach back into our distant human past, we find out who we are as members of the human family. Many things have happened in human history. We find out why they happened and how those things affected the world both in the past and today.

Our Common Needs

All people need the same things to survive, no matter where we live in the world. By studying the past, we have learned that people in the past needed these things too.

- Most important, we need water and food. We get food either by hunting and gathering in the wild or by growing plants.
- We need a way to clothe ourselves.
- We need somewhere to live—a place to shelter us from the cold, heat, wind, and rain.
- We need safety from danger.
- We also need things to look forward to, things that give our lives hope and meaning. For example, you probably have a special event that you look forward to—maybe your birthday or a favourite holiday.

We often use the word *need* to describe things that we want, and we usually can come up with a very long list. But "need" and "want" are two different things. The list of things we really need is very short.

Only when we are safe are we free to take care of our other needs. What two methods of protection do these drawings show us?

The Tools and Methods We Use

When we look back at the early days of human life, it seems amazing that we have come so far. As our population has grown, we have always found ways to live together—both within our communities, and with the other communities in the world. To help us live together, and to help us meet our needs, we use many tools and methods.

Technology

Today's **technology** has its roots in the first discoveries and inventions humans made. The discovery of fire, the wheel, and simple devices like pulleys and levers made possible every discovery that followed. The spread of tools and technologies among people has increased the pace of change in the world and has made the impossible possible for many people.

Laws and Government

In most early societies, powerful rulers were in charge, and religious leaders made the laws. The common people had little say in their lives. Many rulers did try to build a better future for their people through education, fair laws, and order.

Today, governments and organizations around the world share the task of solving global problems. Through **democracy**, many people now have a say in the decisions that affect them.

Technologies are the tools we make and use.

Democracy is a form of government in which power lies with the people, who vote to elect representatives.

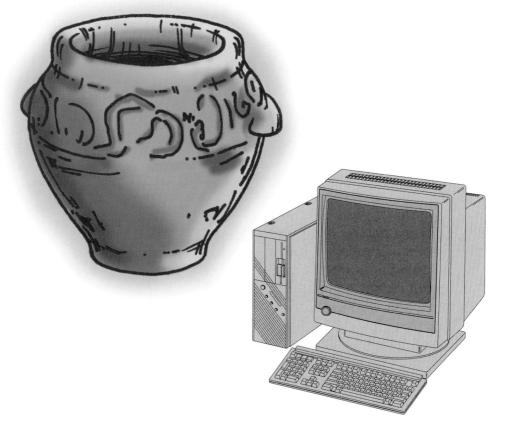

How are an ancient clay pot and a computer the same? Practically everything in your life is a technology. For example, the spoon you use to eat your morning cereal is a technology. So is the word-processing program you use to write a story.

Trade

In ancient times, most people traded only with nearby neighbours. Eventually, trading with far-off communities began, and it brought many benefits. People learned new ideas and acquired different foods, goods, and tools. Bringing grains and other foods from far-off lands quickly expanded a society's ability to feed itself.

Today we live in a **global marketplace**. That means we can trade the goods we make for goods made practically anywhere. We buy and sell to trading partners all over the world to keep our **economy** healthy and to benefit from the variety of goods we receive.

Communications

People have always found ways to share information. In the early days, messages were passed by word of mouth from person to person. Getting messages to people far away usually meant a long journey. In Africa, drumbeats were used to send long-distance messages. Written language was first recorded on clay, stone, leather, and plant fibres.

Today we use electronic communication—**e-mail**—to connect in seconds with people all over the world, and even with astronauts in space. By using computers connected to the **Internet** in homes, workplaces, schools, and libraries, most Canadians can tap into huge stores of knowledge and expertise.

A country's economy is its wealth and resources.

The Internet is a vast computer network with information from governments, businesses, and universities.

Try This

Meet with a partner to find and talk about at least five pieces of evidence that support the statement, "The roots of the present are deep in the past." The examples may be from this chapter or from your own lives. When you have finished, compare your evidence with that of another pair of students.

A Closer Look

Speech

If someone were to ask you the question written to the right, you wouldn't know how to answer it unless you read Hindi. But if Hindi is your **first language**—the language your family spoke to you when you were a small child—you would know that it means "Where do we come from?" Nearly everyone on earth shares the very important ability to communicate by speaking. We all understand at least one language, no matter what race we are or where we were born.

How did we get this skill? Humans developed the skill over thousands of years. It began with early humans, who probably communicated with one another by gesturing and making simple sounds. We still use some of those gestures. Just think of the signs you use to tell someone to *come here, stop,* or *look at this.*

हम कहाँ से आये?

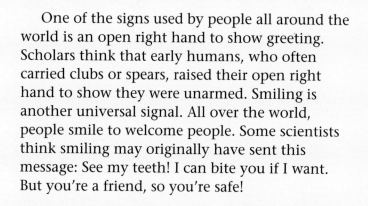

One of the signs used by people all around the world is an open right hand to show greeting. Scholars think that early humans, who often carried clubs or spears, raised their open right hand to show they were unarmed. Smiling is another universal signal. All over the world, people smile to welcome people. Some scientists think smiling may originally have sent this message: See my teeth! I can bite you if I want. But you're a friend, so you're safe!

Old Problems

Despite the many tools and methods we have to help us meet our needs, today we still face some of the same problems faced by those who lived long before us. As in the past, many people are homeless. Some don't have jobs, so they cannot support themselves. War rages in many countries. People still suffer from diseases, even those for which we know the cure. And just as they did in the past, many people wake up in the morning with nothing to eat.

Not Enough to Eat

The problem of not enough food has been central in the human story. People have gone hungry throughout world history. Besides the written records telling us about ancient hunger, scientists have found evidence in the bones of **prehistoric** people showing that many of them were very poorly nourished.

Today, one out of four people in the world does not have enough to eat. Millions of people around the world face a lack of food every day. This lack of food may be **malnutrition**. A malnourished person has some food, but never enough or never the right kind. The lack of food might come in the form of a **famine**. This large-scale emergency occurs when a whole community has absolutely no food to eat.

Overpopulation and other natural or human causes can result in hunger. Natural causes include disasters such as insect plagues, unseasonably cold weather, extreme rainfall, flooding, and drought. Human causes of hunger include wars and poor **food distribution**. Even with plenty of food, countries need practical ways to get food to their people. They need roads, trucks, trains, shopping markets, and refrigeration.

A humanitarian worker in Guatemala carries food supplies across a makeshift bridge.

Pre means "before," so *prehistory* means "before history." We have no written records—and no written histories—of the vast period of time before humans began to write.

Famine comes from the Latin word *fames*, meaning "hunger."

Warfare always causes the worst famines; besides destroying food supplies, it destroys a country's ability to get food to people.

Long ago, societies didn't have many ways to help starving people. What ways do we now have to help people who don't have enough to eat?

At current rates, the earth's population won't level off until after 2100. How big will the population be then? Do you think food production will be able to keep up?

Here are some examples of hunger through time and around the world.

- The ancient stories of Mesopotamia and Egypt feature many famines. A flood or drought could easily cause starvation if the rulers had not stored enough food for rough times.

- Overpopulation has led to serious famines in China and India since 1700. In the years 1876–79 alone, about 13 million people died of starvation in China.

- In Ireland, during the 1840s, the potato crop failed year after year. At least one million people died because the potato was the main source of food. Thousands of people left Ireland to go to other parts of the world in search of better lives.

- Guatemala is a low-income country with little food for its people. The country is still recovering from a 36-year civil war. Many humanitarian agencies work hard to stop people from dying of starvation.

- In Canada in 1999, approximately 744 000 families lived in poverty. Many of these families had little food to eat because it costs a lot of money to live in a country like Canada.

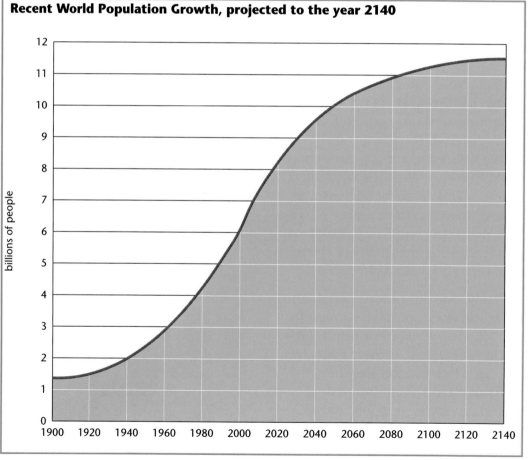

Recent World Population Growth, projected to the year 2140

(vertical axis: billions of people, 0–12; horizontal axis: years 1900–2140)

Yes, There Is Hope!

When we look at our world and think about how we are doing in meeting our basic needs, we see that many of the problems that affected us in the past still affect us today.

There are signs of hope, however. Some problems have been solved, and we're finding more solutions every day. Our world is filled with individuals, communities, nations, and international agencies all trying to figure out good solutions. Read the information that follows to identify some of the solutions people are working on to address the problem of world hunger.

Solutions to World Hunger

The solutions to world hunger involve technology, education, and social activism.

Modern farming technology means that every nation should be able to feed its citizens adequately. For example, in the past 40–50 years, farmers have been getting more and more milk from their dairy cattle. By breeding cows that naturally provide more milk, by keeping them healthy, and by providing them with better nutrition, farmers now have cows that produce more milk than cows did in the past.

How does the technology shown in this picture allow farmers to keep more dairy cows than they did in the past?

Some people argue that **biotechnology** (altering plants and animals genetically) is not a good answer to the problem of hunger. They say that genetically altered products may be dangerous to people's health and the environment.

To increase crop production, scientists have been redesigning plants for special purposes. For example, scientists have discovered that hens use a lot of energy to produce the shell around the egg. They want to find a way to get hens to lay eggs without shells so that they can use the energy to lay more eggs. Even if scientists are successful, however, they may still have a problem. After all, would you buy an egg without a shell?

International agencies such as the Food and Agriculture Organization (FAO) and the World Health Organization (WHO) of the United Nations (UN) are at work helping people in developing countries improve their methods of farming.

Social activists tackle the problem from another direction. For example, some groups are fighting to get the land back to the people. The vast plantations that grow crops to sell outside a country make a few people rich but do not feed the people. By returning the land to small farmers, more people can feed themselves.

This graph shows how many kilograms of grain are needed to make one kilogram of bread or one kilogram of meat. The world's population has doubled in the past 50 years, but we now consume four times as much meat. How does this trend affect the world's ability to feed people?

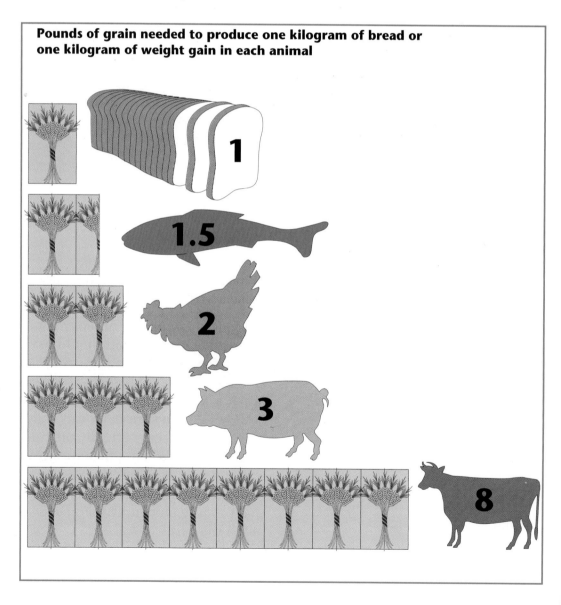

Pounds of grain needed to produce one kilogram of bread or one kilogram of weight gain in each animal

1

1.5

2

3

8

PERSPECTIVES

Solving World Hunger

The two opinions here are responses to the question, "What is the best way to solve the problem of world hunger?" After you have read the two opposing views, decide which one provides the best argument.

Opinion 1: Solving Hunger from the Inside

Giving food aid to the world's hungry helps no one in the long run. To really make a difference, we have to help developing nations gain the skills they need to solve their own problems. We should help farmers learn to use better farming techniques, which would help them grow more crops. Education programs could help new mothers learn what foods their children need. We could help train workers so that they can get jobs and support themselves and their families. Only through these long-term solutions can hunger be defeated.

Opinion 2: Solving Hunger from the Outside

When foreign governments give food aid to starving nations, everyone benefits. Most important, you stop people from dying of starvation. The countries that receive the aid often look to the donor countries for leadership. They see the value of democratic government and try to change their own governments to this model. After they become stronger, developing countries can become trading partners with the donor nations. If all nations were freed from poverty and malnutrition, the world would be a more stable place.

These two photographs show two different ways of coping with the problem of hunger. Above, a Honduran farmer explains the situation to a Canadian farmer who has volunteered his expertise. At right, a Canadian soldier loads up food aid going to Honduras. How does each strategy help?

HOW TO... Talk About Issues

An issue is a debatable subject. That means that two people can have very different views about it. When you talk about an issue, you give your **opinion**—what you think about it. To convince other people of your opinion, you should always explain yourself. The best opinion is always the one with the best reasons supporting it. To know the best reasons, you need to have complete information. When you understand all sides of an issue, then you can make an **informed opinion**.

Preparing to Talk About an Issue

1. *Write a statement to clearly define the issue.* "The issue is…" You may want to revise this statement when you gain more information.

2. *Find out everything you can about the issue.* Try to answer all the questions you can think of about the issue. Who else thinks it is an issue? Why do they think so? Who is affected by it? How are they affected by it?

3. *Decide on what your opinion will be.* To organize your reasoning, you might want to use the planning frame below.

Think "Yes"	Think "No"
List all the ideas and opinions you can think of that support the statement.	List all the ideas and opinions you can think of that oppose the statement.
Write your opinion and give your reasons for having that point of view. Remember to support your view with evidence.	
Think about some of the arguments someone from the opposing point of view might have. Explain why these ideas will not work as well as yours.	
Explain what you would like to see happen and how it might be achieved.	

Talking About an Issue

1. *Be respectful of others.* When you talk about issues with other students, remember that everyone has a right to his or her opinion. Talking with people who hold different views can become a problem when someone gets angry. To avoid this, express your opinion in respectful ways. That way, everyone can benefit—different views are studied, ways of thinking are challenged, and new ideas are formed.

Think For Yourself

What is your opinion? Pick one of the following statements and decide if you agree or disagree with it.

"Rich nations should give enough aid money to end world hunger."

"Technology is the key to solving all the world's problems."

Give reasons to support your opinion. Use How to Talk About Issues to help you form an opinion and get ready for a discussion.

Looking Back

In this chapter you had a chance to think about some of the ways that we, as humans, are connected to the past. We each have our individual pasts, and together we share a collective past. Today, we still face many of the challenges once faced by our ancestors. How do you think knowledge of the past can make us better human beings?

Chapter 2

Puzzling Pieces

*L*et's say a private eye was trying to find out about your recent past. Believe it or not, an excellent source of helpful evidence would be the trash basket in your room. A private eye could find **artifacts**, such as a candy-bar wrapper or the packaging for a computer game. These objects are artifacts because humans made them. Artifacts teach us about the society in which they were made and the person who used them—in this case, you.

It is more difficult for us to find out about the ancient past. Unlike you, people from ancient cultures left very little evidence. We have human skeletons, fragments of bone, and broken tools, but little else. Amazingly, archaeologists learn a great deal about ancient people from these few artifacts and human remains.

In this chapter you can discover the techniques scientists use to uncover evidence about the past and to piece it together to create a realistic picture of life in ancient times.

Artifacts: Pieces of the Past

Have you ever found something that made you really curious about what it was? Maybe it was a button that you didn't recognize, or a foreign coin. You probably figured out some of its past by its colour or style. You might have guessed what kind of person could have owned it. After that, you were probably left with a mystery because you had no other evidence.

well as natural materials such as the bones of animals and humans. Most evidence is broken or in pieces, such as pottery **shards**. A hundred years ago, archaeologists might have had only the physical remains and their imagination to work with. Today, archaeologists also use advanced technology to find and analyze evidence. For example, they can study satellite photographs of ancient sites.

Archaeology comes from the Greek word *arkhaiologia*. It means the "study of ancient things."

Archaeologists

Archaeologists are often left with similar mysteries. Archaeologists are the scientists who collect and study the remains of past human activity. They work with other scientists to try to explain what life was like for ancient peoples. The evidence archaeologists work with includes items ancient people used or made such as stone tools and pottery, as

Archaeologists find shards, or pieces of broken pottery, more often than they find any other type of evidence of the past.

This artifact shows what one ancient person considered important.

Archaeologists found this painting of a wild horse hidden deep in a cave in southwestern France. They decided it was painted about 17 000 years ago, long before written history. What reasons could the ancient artist have had for creating this particular picture?

A hypothesis is the best guess a person can make when trying to find the answer to a question.

Archaeologists try to make sense of their discoveries—or interpret them—by examining each piece and by putting various pieces together to see if they make sense. They cannot learn about past societies from written records because prehistoric peoples didn't keep any. Instead, archaeologists depend on their specialized skills in analyzing artifacts and human remains.

Thinking Like an Archaeologist

Archaeologists begin their analysis of an artifact by making an initial guess, or **hypothesis**, about its purpose or significance. They test their hypothesis and look for additional evidence to prove that their interpretation is right or wrong. Archaeologists use many different methods to locate and assess evidence.

HOW TO... Make Hypotheses

Ask yourself, "Why does our classroom have rules?"

To make sure we all feel safe, I guess!

?

So we won't be too noisy?

So we can get our work done.

What other answers would you suggest? Pick the one you think is probably the best answer. That's your hypothesis. You can use the steps on the following page to make and test any hypothesis.

1. *Define the question.* What do you want to know? Which question do you think you could answer and then prove? It helps to be specific. Instead of, "What was life like for ancient Mayans?" try "What did ancient Mayans usually eat?"

2. *Collect evidence.* Make notes about what you already know. Research using a variety of sources. Ask others what they know about the topic. As you get new information, check back to see if your question needs adjusting. You might try something more specific, like, "What did ancient Mayans eat for breakfast?"

3. *Examine the evidence.* Analyze the information in your notes. Organize the ideas under headings. Decide how you might summarize the ideas. Speculate about the meaning of the evidence in front of you. As you get new thoughts, check back to see if you should change your question.

4. *Make a hypothesis.* Use the ideas you have collected and examined to make an educated guess of the best answer. Write your educated guess in a sentence that begins like this one: "My hypothesis is that Mayans usually ate pizza for breakfast."

5. *Test your hypothesis.* You can test your hypothesis by experimenting, getting more information, or using common sense. For example, common sense should tell you that Mayans did not eat pizza at all, let alone for breakfast. Time to adjust your hypothesis!

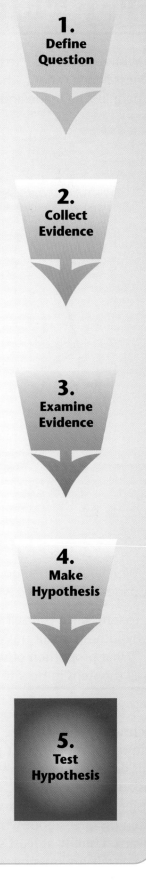

1.
Define
Question

2.
Collect
Evidence

3.
Examine
Evidence

4.
Make
Hypothesis

5.
Test
Hypothesis

Try This

1. With a partner, discuss the artifacts illustrated below. **Speculate** (think of possibilities) about what they are and what they tell you about the lives of the people who made and used them. **Justify** your hypotheses to a partner.

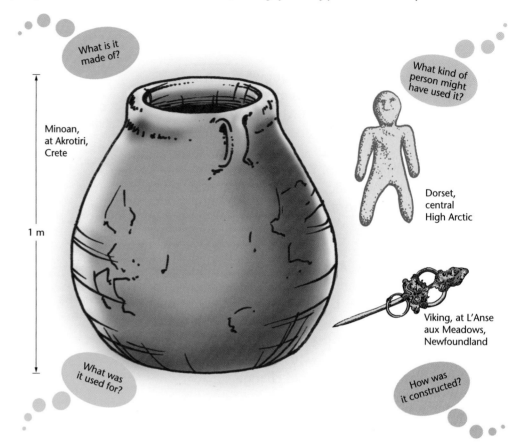

What is it made of?

What kind of person might have used it?

Minoan, at Akrotiri, Crete

1 m

Dorset, central High Arctic

Viking, at L'Anse aux Meadows, Newfoundland

What was it used for?

How was it constructed?

With your partner, go over the steps in How to Make Hypotheses on pages 24–25 to see which steps you used.

2. To familiarize yourself with the steps of making a hypothesis, make and test a hypothesis about trash baskets. Begin by thinking of a question—for example, "What proportion of students have a trash basket in their rooms?" Then follow all the steps in How to Make Hypotheses.

Scientists use very sophisticated technologies to analyze the artifacts and remains of ancient peoples. But this does not necessarily make the task of interpreting the evidence any easier. In fact, different scientists often disagree about what evidence means. Usually at least some pieces of the puzzle are missing, so each scientist may have a different explanation about the missing pieces.

All archaeologists agree that the more evidence we have, the closer we can come to a realistic picture of the past. The next section of this chapter tells you more about ways that archaeologists find and analyze artifacts.

Digging Up the Past

Treasures in Trash

Just as a private eye would find useful information about you in your trash basket, so do archaeologists find information about ancient people in their garbage dumps! Many remains are found in the trash left in early settlement sites or on the floors of caves. Here excavators find the bones of animals people have eaten. They also find artifacts such as broken and discarded tools, furniture, jewellery, and pottery. From their studies of these remains, archaeologists speculate about the lives of these early humans and how they used materials from the environment.

The Dig

Archaeologists find most of their evidence buried in the ground. After deciding on a location, they plan an **excavation**, or dig. Every step must be taken in the right order. Archaeologists want to be sure that they don't overlook or destroy any evidence at the site.

As archaeologists excavate a site, they look for layers where the soil has a slightly different colour, texture, or chemical make-up. Each layer shows the influence of different environmental factors or human activities.

What would your family's garbage tell about your life?

As archaeologists dig through the layers, they keep track of where each artifact is located in relation to other artifacts. How the pieces relate to one another is part of the evidence.

Two of the many activities that occur during an excavation can be seen in this photograph taken at Port au Choix National Historic Park in Newfoundland. Working on one well-defined square at a time, these two excavators dig, sift, record, put artifacts into bags, clean the square, and sweep the soil into a small pan. Notice what each person in the photograph is doing.

Excavators use fine brushes and dental probes to uncover objects that are likely to break or disintegrate. Here excavators work at Torcello Island in Venice, Italy. They carefully measure and sketch their finds.

Reading Hint

Not sure how to say a difficult word? Just follow the pronunciation guides like this one for Isernia La Pineta. The stress falls on the syllable in capital letters.

Italy

Isernia

This site, near Isernia in central Italy, was discovered during the building of a highway between Naples and Vasto. What is each excavator doing? What other activities might uncover ancient sites?

An Early Site in Europe

Isernia La Pineta [ih-ZAIR-nee-uh lah pee-NAY-tuh] is the earliest known human settlement in Europe. It was first occupied 700 000 years ago. After finding the site, archaeologists had to dig through many layers to find the artifacts.

The Isernia site was located near a river that flooded in rainy years. In some years, nearby volcanoes erupted, spewing ash over the site. These **natural processes** buried garbage and other objects under thick layers of river **silt** (fine sand) and volcanic dust. The layers of silt and dust were each about 5 m deep.

These layers protected the artifacts from the atmosphere and preserved them. As archaeologists dug down through the layers, they found evidence of 14 **habitations**, or human settlements, at various depths.

Archaeologists found plant and animal remains, as well as human artifacts, all in good shape. The evidence includes signs that the people of Isernia hunted, gathered food, made stone tools, and ate **marrow**. Bone marrow is the soft material that fills a bone cavity. How do you think archaeologists knew this material had been eaten?

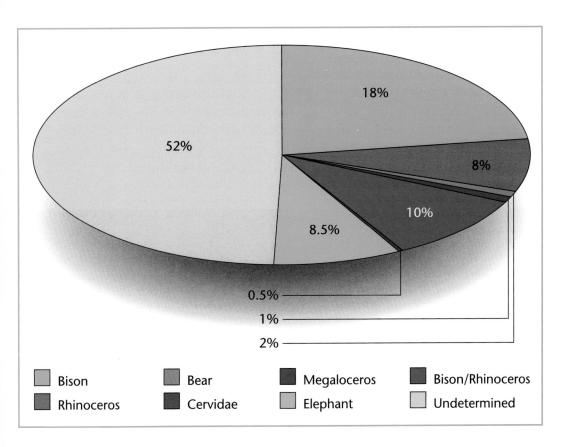

18%

52%

8%

10%

8.5%

0.5%
1%
2%

| Bison | Bear | Megaloceros | Bison/Rhinoceros |
| Rhinoceros | Cervidae | Elephant | Undetermined |

By examining the animal remains found at the Isernia site, archaeologists found proof that the animals had been hunted by humans. They found more plant-eating animals than meat-eating animals, and more older animals than younger ones. Using the legend, figure out which animal was caught and eaten most often.

Try This

Look back over the map, photographs, text, captions, and graph about the archaeological site at Isernia.

1. List three facts about the site. Write two questions you have about how people might have lived in Isernia, Europe's first human settlement.

2. Now, interpret the information by listing ways that the environment influenced the lives of these early people. How did they meet their basic needs? What other information do you need to get a full picture of this society?

Scientific Techniques

After they get the artifacts in hand, archaeologists use many different techniques to gather more information about the artifacts. Here are just a few.

Comparison: Archaeologists compare finds with similar objects found at other sites. For example, if a pot looks just like pots from another region, the two peoples may have been trading.

Statistical analysis: Archaeologists make accurate counts of various types of remains. For example, a large proportion of gazelle bones might indicate that people who lived at the site liked eating gazelle.

Chemical analysis: Using various forms of chemical analysis, archaeologists can figure out many things. For example, a high level of lead in body tissue could indicate that a person died of lead poisoning.

Dating: A common test, **carbon-14 dating**, measures the amount of carbon-14 in an object. Because the amount of carbon-14 decreases over time, scientists can tell when something died.

Remote sensing: Satellites with special equipment can measure light reflecting off the earth's surface. This allows archaeologists to identify previously hidden ancient roads, fields, and buildings.

This aerial photograph reveals the walls of an ancient Roman fortlet in a hayfield in Kirkcudbridgeshire, England. Stone just below the surface caused grass to dry out, thereby revealing the ditches of the fortlet.

A Closer Look

The Laetoli Footprints

Laetoli [la-TOH-lee] lies near an ancient volcano in Tanzania. In ancient times, the volcano erupted and covered the area with hot ash. Shortly afterwards, rain turned the ash to mud. Animals crossing the area left footprints in the wet ash. Three Australopithecus **hominids**—very early humans—also left their footprints. The sun dried the footprints. As more ash fell, the footprints were covered and remained hidden for nearly 4 million years.

In 1976, the famous **anthropologist** Mary Leakey and her team discovered the footprints when they were working in the Laetoli area. (Anthropologists study human beings and human society.) The arrangement of the footprints suggests that they were made by two adults and a child. The shape of the footprints suggests that all three walked upright, as we do. The scientists studied, photographed, and made **casts** (moulds) of the footprints. Leakey decided that they should preserve the footprints so that scientists in the future could analyze them using more advanced technology. The team covered up the prints with five layers of sand and soil, and capped the mound with large boulders.

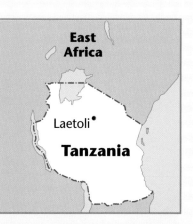

Mary Leakey's team found the Laetoli Footprints in Tanzania, East Africa.

Can you spot all three sets of footprints?

Think For Yourself

Do you think Mary Leakey made a wise decision to cover the footprints? She had two possible courses of action. The first was to leave the site open. The second was to cover the site, which she did.

Experimental Archaeology

Archaeologists use the techniques of modern archaeology to get as much information as possible from their artifacts. Using all their collected evidence, they speculate—or try to make educated guesses—by considering what they know and by using their imagination.

One way they test their guesses is by trying out different explanations to see which ones seem most reasonable. In experimental archaeology, scientists pretend to be the people they are studying. These scientists are like actors taking part in a role-play of ancient times.

To recreate conditions, scientists choose a site with the same climatic conditions as the site they're studying. There they build homes, using the materials available to early people, and then live in them. For props, they make and use tools just like the ones they found at the site. Then they try to meet all their daily needs just as early humans would have done. In this way, scientists can see which of their interpretations work and which do not. They can also pinpoint the gaps in their information. By knowing what they don't know, archaeologists have a better idea about what to look for in future research.

Create a three-column chart to analyze techniques that archaeologists use to find out about the past. List the techniques you find in this section in the first column. In the second column, summarize the usefulness of the technique. In the final column, summarize the limitations of the technique. Add more information to your chart as you read the rest of this chapter.

Ancient Mysteries

Who Were the Amazons?

We've all heard of the Amazons: an ancient tribe of fiercely independent, horse-riding warrior women. They first appear in ancient Greek mythology. Hercules himself conquers Hippolyte [Hip-POL-ee-tee], the Amazon queen, so

he can take her belt, a present given to her by Ares, the God of War. Could these myths be grounded in truth?

We do know about the first people to ride horses. The Scythians [SY-thee-uns] lived on the steppes—the great plains of Central Asia. In a recent discovery, archaeologists found an ancient Scythian graveyard filled with hundreds of graves of horse-riding women warriors. They had been buried with bows and arrows, swords, and armour.

Were these the Amazons of Greek mythology—the legendary women warriors who fought with bow and arrow?

On Greek pottery, the Amazon women warriors were often shown in battle with men. On this vase, an Amazon uses her weapon of choice, the spear.

Renate Rolle, a German archaeologist, has excavated over 100 of the Scythian women's graves. Here is what she found.

They used a bow—it's a good weapon for a woman because you don't need brute strength to use it; all you need is to be fast and flexible. We know they rode horses. Defensive weapons tend to be heavy, but we've found mail-shirts and armour in women's graves, so we know they used them. And some skeletons show signs of the women being wounded in battle.

The artifacts Rolle found at least prove that these women were warriors. We may never know if these warriors were the Amazons of legend.

Putting Pieces Together

Archaeologists and others piece together evidence they have gathered to create a picture of what life was like in a particular time and place. But it is like trying to do a jigsaw puzzle when some of the pieces are missing. To make the picture as complete as possible, archaeologists need to get the maximum amount of information from the evidence they have. The more pieces they can put together, the better the picture they can create.

As you read and view the pictures in "An Amazing Find," notice how the various pieces are put together to make a picture of the Iceman, a man who lived and died in Europe over 5000 years ago.

AN AMAZING FIND

"It's a man!" cried Erika Simon. Erika and her husband, Helmut, bent down to get a closer look at the weathered head and shoulders of a corpse sticking out of the snow.

Gathering the evidence

The Simons' amazing find quickly caught the interest of scientists around the world. The scientists were most interested in the unique circumstances of the victim's death. Some researchers believed that the Iceman froze to death after falling asleep, perhaps while shepherding animals. Some

thought he had been gathering materials to make bows and arrows. Some thought he had been crossing the Alps to trade goods. Other researchers thought he may have died from arsenic poisoning, or from an infection—he did have six broken ribs. At any rate, he died.

Snow must have covered the Iceman's body quickly. It probably froze in a matter of hours. Because the body was locked in the ice, it was saved from being

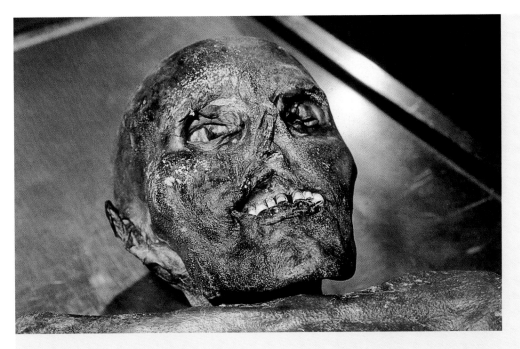

eaten by insects or wild animals. The narrow gully where the Iceman died protected the body from the grinding movements of the glacier that buried it. Here the body lay for thousands of years. Then, during an unusual warming trend in 1991, the glacier shrank, revealing the Iceman.

Archaeologists searched the site carefully to find the Iceman's belongings near his body. When he died, the Iceman had been carrying a wooden axe with a copper blade, a bow and arrows that probably once had feathers on them, a flint dagger, and other hunting tools.

Analyzing the evidence

At first, the scientists thought the Iceman was about 4000 years old. They used various techniques to analyze the body and artifacts and to test their theory. The scientists found out that their estimates of the age of the Iceman were incorrect. By using the scientific method called carbon-14 dating, they found out that the Iceman had died about 5300 years ago.

Putting the pieces together

The evidence that archaeologists gather helps them recreate what life was like for those they are studying. Our picture of the Iceman and what his life might have been like has been carefully pieced together from many clues. For example, consider the Iceman's clothing described at right and shown in the illustration on the next page. What kind of weather do you think the Iceman expected on his journey?

- The Iceman's shoes were oval pieces of leather turned up at the edges and tied with leather straps. A web of knotted grass cords covered his feet. These held in place the grass that was stuffed inside the shoes for warmth.

- He wore a cone-shaped fur cap. It had a leather chinstrap to keep it on his head.

- His upper garment was only partially preserved. It was made of squares of fur sewn together, and may or may not have had sleeves.

- He wore two separate, loose-fitting leggings of a light-brown fur. These were tied to a belt at his waist.

- A braided grass cape gave him more protection. It was tied around his neck and came down to his knees.

Soot was found in the Iceman's lungs. This suggests that he spent considerable time inside a smoky dwelling.

Two barleycorns still in their husks were found in the Iceman's clothing. These suggest that he had recently been somewhere where grain was being harvested.

A single sloe berry found with the Iceman suggests that he died in the early fall, when the berries ripen. Pollen found in the glacier ice supports this hypothesis.

Examination of the Iceman's skull and teeth suggests that he was between 25 and 40 years old.

The roots of the Iceman's hair contained traces of copper and arsenic. This suggests he made copper tools. Another clue was his axe—it had a copper blade.

PERSPECTIVES

Who owns historical artifacts?

Many discoveries made by archaeologists have led to disputes. In the case of the Iceman, a controversy arose about who owned the body and artifacts. When scientists first announced the find, a woman in Europe claimed that the body was that of her father, and she wanted it. The Simons said they owned half. Italy and Austria both claimed the body because it was found in the mountains between their two countries. A close check of the area showed that the body was found in Italy. In 1998, the body was finally returned to Italy, where the Iceman received a hero's welcome to a museum built in his honour.

Who owns historical artifacts and remains ? This is a question asked by people all over the world. People have many different perspectives on this issue.

"Artifacts are of historical and scientific importance. They are part of the heritage of humankind. They belong in museums."

"Artifacts and remains found at burial sites should remain untouched. Their spiritual value matters, not their scientific value. The preservation of ancient spiritual places is most important."

Who should own historical artifacts and remains?

"Artifacts belong in the countries where they were found. Countries should have laws to stop historical artifacts from leaving their lands."

"Artifacts are treasures for whoever finds them. If I'm lucky enough to find an artifact while I travel the world, then I should be able to own it and show it to my friends."

Try This

Write a list of questions you would like to ask the Iceman.

With a partner, use your questions to present a television interview between a TV talk-show host and the Iceman. Make up an interesting name for your TV talk show and use it in your introduction.

Think For Yourself

1. Do you think people should spend money and make the effort to examine the Iceman and his belongings? What would be the short- and long-term consequences of acting on your position? Is this a worthwhile effort? Be prepared to give reasons to support your position.

2. Compare the pros and cons of keeping artifacts in a museum and leaving them at a site. To collect your ideas, make a two-column table with the headings "Advantages of putting artifacts in a museum" and "Advantages of keeping artifacts at their site." State your reasons clearly. Consider both sides of the problem. Then write a statement that proposes a solution to the problem.

What Do We Know?

History is the study of change over time. Studying history helps us understand how all cultures are influenced by the changing environment. We also learn how different peoples developed skills over time.

CE stands for the Common Era, which includes all years after and including Year 1. BCE stands for Before the Common Era.

Neolithic people made Stonehenge on the Salisbury Plain in Britain around 2550 **BCE**. Most evidence indicates that the builders moved the huge bluestones from a site 240 km away. New evidence suggests that the stones may have been moved by glaciers. Though not convinced, few scientists rule out this possibility. Instead, they wait for more evidence to appear.

What we know for sure about early humans is really very little. We speculate on the bits and pieces of evidence that we find. With these we try to piece together the story of humankind. And as new evidence is found, we change our idea of what life was like.

For example, at one time humans knew nothing of the dinosaurs that roamed the earth for millions of years. Then the remains of dinosaurs were discovered, so we began to picture an ancient history in which humans hid in caves from Tyrannosaurus Rex, and hunted Diploducus [dih-PLAH-duh-kus]. New evidence, however, proved that the dinosaurs died out long before humans walked the earth. So scientists revised their beliefs about early human life once again.

Scientists answer their questions by interpreting the evidence available to them. They justify their interpretations by giving facts or reasons that explain the evidence they have. But scientists do not accept any idea as proven for all time. As they uncover more evidence and use new technologies, they justify new interpretations.

Hypotheses About Human Beginnings

Two widely held hypotheses about the origin of humans are **creationism** and **evolution**. For hundreds of years, scholars and scientists have been energetically debating these positions. Both hypotheses address the question of where humans come from.

PERSPECTIVES

The Origin of Humans

Evolution

Human evolution is a scientific theory that explains the origin and development of the human species. According to theories of **evolution**, simple forms of life change gradually, over many generations, into more complex forms of life.

Scientists believe that human-like beings first populated the earth about four million years ago. Many believe that humans developed from a simpler, ape-like species.

Although scientists may disagree on various aspects of ancient life, most believe the theory of evolution because it is based on scientific observation of evidence.

Creationism

Creationism is the belief that the universe and everything in it was created by a divine being. Many people have faith that this is true. Many see no conflict between this belief and the processes of evolution described by science. They believe that God created the processes of evolution along with everything else.

Virtually every culture on earth has a creation story that explains the creation of the earth, of plants and animals, and of human beings. These explanations reveal and strengthen our beliefs, values, customs, and rules for society. They help us know who we are.

Ancient Stories

The Mayan Creation Story

Over 2000 years ago, the Maya developed a complex civilization with a far-reaching network of trade. They built stunning buildings, including pyramids, and developed a calendar using their knowledge of astronomy. They also developed a system of writing. The following is a version of a creation story from one of their books, the Popol Vuh [POH-pul VUH].

Before creation there were no people, animals, birds, fish, crabs, trees, or stones. There was only a calm sea. The creators, K'ucumatiz [koo-koo-MAH-teez] and Tepew [TEE-pyoo], first made the earth with its mountains, plains, and rivers and then made animals like deer, jaguar, and snakes. The creators assigned each animal its own place to live in the newly created world.

The creators next ordered the animals to speak so that they might praise the creators for their work; the animals, however, could not speak. The creators then decided to make creatures that could; these would be people. The first people, made of mud, could speak, but they had no minds and merely dissolved in the water. Then the creators made people out of wood. The people multiplied and spread across the earth. They could speak, but they lacked blood and minds, and they did not remember the creators who made them. K'ucumatiz and Tepew ordered that they be destroyed; birds plucked out their eyes, and jaguars devoured their woody flesh. Some of these wooden men nevertheless managed to escape into the jungle, where all that remains of them today are the monkeys.... This is why monkeys are similar to human beings.

Finally, the fox, the coyote, the parrot, and the crow told the creators about the yellow and white corn that grew on the earth. The creators ground and mixed the yellow and white corn; from this cornmeal, they made the flesh and blood of the first true people. These people had blood and minds, and they worshipped the gods who created them and the world in which they lived.

From Kenneth Feder and Michael Park, *Human Antiquity*, (Toronto: Mayfield Publishing Company, 1992), 5–7

Parrot tells one of the Mayan creator beings about corn. The creator then makes the first true people out of corn meal.

Investigate

Work with a small group to present a story about the creation of earth, animals, or people. You may want to use the Maya story from your text, or you may decide to find a different story. Your presentation could be a skit, a puppet play, a dramatic reading, or a series of **tableaux** [ta-BLOH] (frozen scenes).

Looking Back

In this chapter you looked at the techniques of archaeology. You saw how archaeology helps us learn about and understand what life was like for ancient people. What do you think is the most important role of the archaeologist?

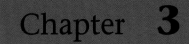

Steps to Civilization

ook around you. How did the world you see come to be the way it is? Why are you reading a book instead of lying in wait outside a gopher's hole, with a spiked club in your hands?

Yes, we have other ways of getting dinner these days. The reason we do lies far in the past, when early humans began creating tools to help them make useful and beautiful objects. People began farming instead of spending their days searching for food. They left their caves for the comfort of houses built from reeds, peat, leather, wood, and stone. They built walls around their settlements, and began to live peacefully in settled communities. These early changes were the first steps towards civilization, and the first steps towards the life we know.

In this chapter you can examine these important changes in the lives of early humans, changes that affected the lives of all the people who followed them, including you!

Early Beginnings

Judging by the map, which group of humans was the biggest "world traveller"?

Archaeologists have found evidence showing that at least six different species of humans have walked the earth. These include the first modern humans, the early *Homo sapiens sapiens* [HOH-moh SAY-pyenz SAY-pyenz]. On the map below, you can find out where and when each species **flourished** (thrived).

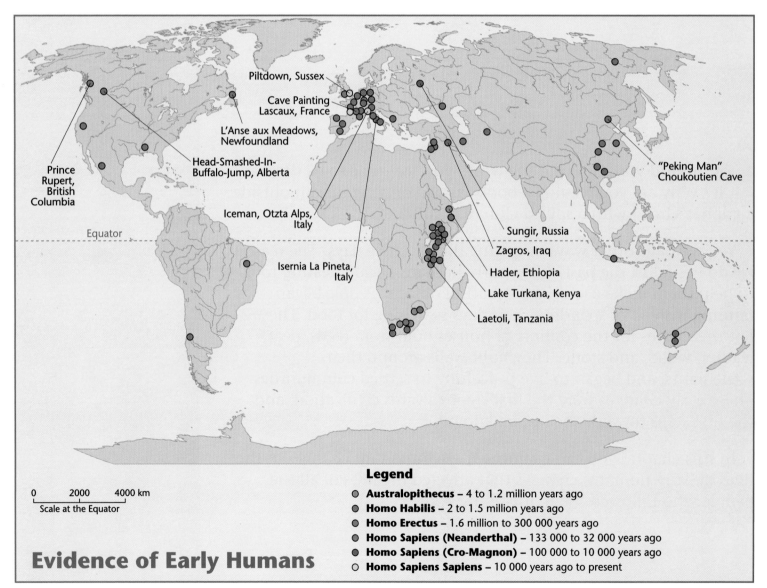

Piltdown, Sussex

Cave Painting Lascaux, France

L'Anse aux Meadows, Newfoundland

Head-Smashed-In-Buffalo-Jump, Alberta

Prince Rupert, British Columbia

Iceman, Otzta Alps, Italy

Equator

Isernia La Pineta, Italy

"Peking Man" Choukoutien Cave

Sungir, Russia

Zagros, Iraq

Hader, Ethiopia

Lake Turkana, Kenya

Laetoli, Tanzania

0   2000   4000 km
Scale at the Equator

Evidence of Early Humans

Legend

- ● **Australopithecus** – 4 to 1.2 million years ago
- ● **Homo Habilis** – 2 to 1.5 million years ago
- ● **Homo Erectus** – 1.6 million to 300 000 years ago
- ● **Homo Sapiens (Neanderthal)** – 133 000 to 32 000 years ago
- ● **Homo Sapiens (Cro-Magnon)** – 100 000 to 10 000 years ago
- ○ **Homo Sapiens Sapiens** – 10 000 years ago to present

Read Maps

Maps give you tools to help you read them. Here are three.

Title. Many maps have titles. Sometimes these appear in the legend box or in a caption. The title tells you what information the map contains.

Legend. Another tool is the map legend. This provides the code for the map. It shows what various colours and symbols on the map represent.

Scale. The map scale tells you how distance on the map is related to the actual distance on earth. For example, a **ratio scale** tells you how many times bigger the distance on earth would be. A ratio scale of 1:40 000 tells you that 1 inch on the map equals 40 000 inches on the earth. A **bar scale**, or linear scale, actually *shows* you the relationship. The number underneath the bar, or line, tells you what distance is represented by the length of bar shown. A bar scale like the one here tells us that a distance on the map equal to the length of the bar represents 600 km on the earth.

▬▬▬▬▬

600 km

Try This

Find the title, legend, and scale of the map on the previous page. What information does each of these items give you? Describe where the remains of the six groups of ancient humans were located in relation to major rivers. What pattern do you notice?

Think For Yourself

Imagine yourself shipwrecked on a deserted island. Your mission is to survive on your wits alone. Your first task is to find food and water. You gather shellfish from the beach and find a stream. What now? Work with a small group to speculate on the following.

- You see some fruit, but it is high up in a tree. Can you create a tool from available materials to help you solve this problem? Describe it.

- You want to bring some water back to the beach. Can you make a tool for carrying and storing water? Describe it.

- Brainstorm a list of short- and long-term needs for living on the deserted isle. What tools can you create from available materials? Explain how each tool helps you meet a short- or long-term need.

Development of Humans

By examining the tools of ancient peoples, we learn how they hunted and what they hunted (small or large prey). We learn how they cooked their food (on a spit, for example) and if they stored it.

Why do you think we call our own era the Computer Age?

Fossils form when the remains of plants or animals change into rock, or when a plant or animal leaves an impression (like a footprint).

For early humans, the earth was much like a deserted island. It offered the materials of nature, but nothing else. People survived by finding ways to use these materials to meet their need for food, shelter, and clothing. For example, they made axes, knives, scrapers, and spearheads by using a hard stone to chip pieces from another stone. Various groups of humans created different tools, depending on their environment. Ancient tools tell us a lot about what each group's life was like.

As people learned how to make new tools out of different materials, their lives changed drastically. Scientists have divided up the time when early humans lived into three **eras**, or periods of time. We use the names **Stone Age**, **Bronze Age**, and **Iron Age** for the periods when people used tools made of these materials.

On the following few pages, you'll see illustrations and evidence of six different groups of humans. According to the theory of evolution, each of these species of humans developed into the next group. Some groups lived on earth at the same time, as you can see by looking at the time line.

Scientists do not all agree on the names and dates for each group of early humans. They support their different hypotheses about the existence of each group by analyzing **fossil** remains. Most archaeologists agree with the hypotheses described on the following pages. As you read, pay attention to how scientists believe each species of early humans used technology to help them survive in their environment.

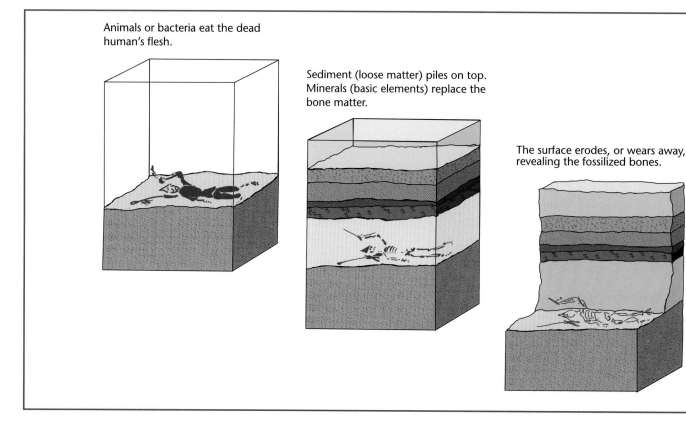

Animals or bacteria eat the dead human's flesh.

Sediment (loose matter) piles on top. Minerals (basic elements) replace the bone matter.

The surface erodes, or wears away, revealing the fossilized bones.

Australopithecus (southern ape)
Approximately 1.2 to 4 million years ago

Scientists call *Australopithecus* [ah-struh-loh-PIH-thih-kus] a "prehuman hominoid," which means that they were not fully like human. The study of their fossilized skeletons suggests that they were apelike, but walked on two legs instead of four. They had small brains, and teeth similar to today's humans.

Australopithecus could use only the simplest tools. For example, they might push a twig into an anthill, and then pull it out covered in ants.

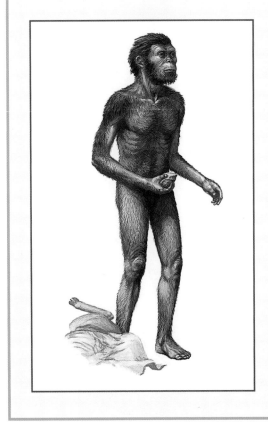

Homo habilis (handyman)
2 to 1.5 million years ago

Scientists consider *Homo habilis* [HOH-mo HAH-bee-lis] the first real human. The length of the bone fossils shows that these people walked upright with long, dangling arms. Other evidence suggests that they made crude shelters from branches and used stones as tools. For this reason, archaeologists nicknamed *Homo habilis* "handyman." Though not skillful hunters, these humans did eat meat if they found discarded carcasses.

By knocking stone flakes off of hard stones, *Homo habilis* produced tools for chopping, scraping, and cutting. What would these humans want to chop, scrape, and cut?

Homo erectus (upright man)
1.6 million to 80 000 years ago

Homo erectus [HOH-moh ee-REK-tus] looked more like us than earlier humans did. They were as tall as we are, but they were stronger. Measurements of the skull cavity suggest that *Homo erectus* had a bigger brain than *Homo habilis*, but they could not talk. Other evidence indicates that "upright man" had learned how to make fire.

Homo erectus could make complex tools, including a hand axe and tools for butchering. These tools allowed *Homo erectus* to hunt game from Africa to Asia.

Homo sapiens (Neanderthal)
133 000 to 32 000 years ago

Sapiens means "thinking." Early *Homo sapiens*, commonly known as Neanderthals [nee-AN-der-thals], were smarter than earlier humans. Their remains and the items they left behind suggest that they made stone knives, a process that takes nine steps and about 250 blows. Neanderthals built shelters and other structures to protect themselves. Some scientists say that these were the first people to bury their dead.

Besides making stone knives, Neanderthals also made throwing weapons such as harpoons and spears.

Homo sapiens (Cro-Magnon)
100 000 to 10 000 years ago

Cro-Magnon [kroh-MAG-nun] humans, another group of *Homo sapiens*, had even bigger brains and a real capacity for complex thinking. Cro-Magnons are named after the place where they were first found, in France. Evidence found in caves there suggests that Cro-Magnons invented a variety of tools to hunt and fish, paint and draw, sew, make music, and fight with others. Cro-Magnon humans made both fish hooks and needles from antlers.

Cro-Magnon burial sites contained objects such as beads, fur garments, and ivory jewellery. This suggests that Cro-Magnon lived, at least part of the year, in a settled community.

Homo sapiens sapiens (modern humans)
10 000 years ago to the present

Homo sapiens sapiens is the species to which modern-day people belong. Evidence of these humans first appeared in Africa. By virtue of their superior tool-making skills, these modern humans survived the last Ice Age and went on to populate the earth. Only with *Homo sapiens sapiens* did human civilization finally become possible.

Besides precisely made tools, modern humans developed their tool-making skills in other areas—for example, by weaving baskets from reeds.

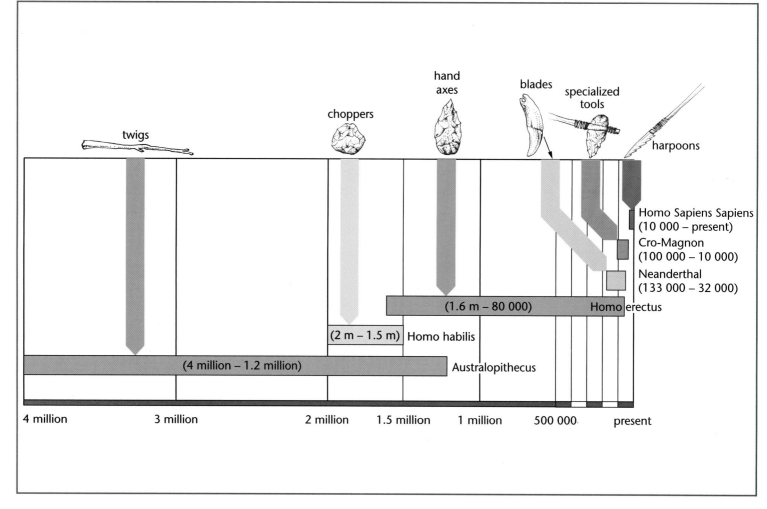

twigs

choppers

hand axes

blades

specialized tools

harpoons

Homo Sapiens Sapiens (10 000 – present)
Cro-Magnon (100 000 – 10 000)
Neanderthal (133 000 – 32 000)
(1.6 m – 80 000) Homo erectus
(2 m – 1.5 m) Homo habilis
(4 million – 1.2 million) Australopithecus

4 million   3 million   2 million   1.5 million   1 million   500 000   present

This time line shows when each of the six major human species lived on earth. How would you describe the length of time that modern humans, *Homo sapiens sapiens*, has existed compared with how long the other human species lived here?

Try This

1. Using the material on the previous pages, choose either (a) *activities and inventions* of ancient humans or (b) *skills* of ancient humans and write a list of the changes that took place from *Australopithecus* to *Homo sapiens sapiens*. List the changes on a time line.

2. Make a list of the tools that each of the groups of people created and used. Speculate on at least two ways that each tool changed the lives of the people who created them.

Hunting and Gathering

Early Hunters

In ancient times, people could not be certain of getting dinner if they stayed in one place. People ate wild plants when they were in season. They ate the wild animals they could catch and kill with tools of wood and stone. They followed migrating herds of animals, or travelled to places where they had found food in past years. Hunting was a way of life for early humans. Evidence found at many sites suggests that early humans—starting with *Homo erectus*—were skillful hunters.

What are the advantages and disadvantages of the hunter-gatherer lifestyle?

North American Aboriginal people stampeded herds of bison off cliffs such as the one at Head-Smashed-in-Buffalo-Jump, Alberta. Why do you think this hunting method encouraged people to live in communities?

This scene shows what archaeologists think happened at a site in Italy about 70 000 years ago. According to their evidence, a group of Neanderthal hunters first caught an elephant in a pit. Then they killed it with stone-tipped spears. Notice what each hunter is doing. What evidence in the picture suggests that the hunters are experienced?

Ancient humans used wood, bone, and plant fibres to make tools. Most of these materials rotted, leaving little or no evidence. Only stone tools survived.

Cro-Magnon Hunters

Cro-Magnon people followed the great herds of animals that once travelled across Europe. Some lived in caves. Others made tents out of the skins of the animals they caught. They could pack up tents easily and bring them along as they followed the herds of animals. The tools made by Cro-Magnon humans were much more efficient than those of earlier people. They invented blade tools and made tools from bone to help them make clothing and shelters.

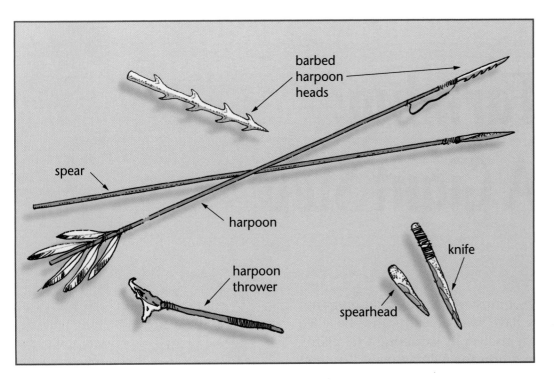

The invention of the barbed harpoon was important to the growth of population. Hunting became more efficient as the hunting tools improved. Notice the details of the spears and harpoons shown here. How do you think these tools would make hunting more efficient?

Try This

Make a three-column chart to summarize how early hunters and gatherers satisfied their needs, and to compare this with how we satisfy our needs today. Begin by listing, in the left column, the following needs: food and water, shelter, clothing, safety, and a sense of belonging.

Investigate

Putting yourself into the time and place of an historical event can help you investigate an idea. Imagine that you are one of a band of early humans who travel together in search of food:

You eat roots, fruit, and berries whenever you find them. You eat raw meat because you do not know about fire. You break animal bones open so you can eat the marrow. Then one day you see fire for the first time. How does the fire start? How does it change your life? What can you do now that you could not do before?

Work in a group to develop a cartoon strip, short skit, or mural about your discovery of fire. First recreate the occasion when you discovered fire for the first time. Then show how you learned to use it for various purposes related to food, tools, shelter, and safety.

Farming: A Giant Step

By 5000 years ago, people had begun farming in almost every part of the world that had moderate temperatures, enough rainfall, and fertile soil.

"Food production—the deliberate cultivation of food-plants, especially cereals, and the taming, breeding, and selection of animals—was an economic revolution—the greatest in human history after the mastery of fire."
– *V. Gordon Childe*

If you found plants growing on a spot where you had spilled grain, what conclusion would you come to?

For most of the time that humans have lived on earth, they have fed themselves by gathering wild plants and hunting wild animals. Farming marks the time when people began to grow plants and raise animals for food. They also began training animals to be of use to them. The switch to farming marks a gigantic change in how people related to the earth and their environment. Instead of simply finding and taking what nature provided, people started to help nature along. As farmers, humans started to take control of the production of food.

This shift from food gathering to food producing meant that people could now be sure of getting enough to eat. A dependable source of food allowed people to settle in one place. As food became abundant, communities began to flourish. Farming was a giant step towards the development of civilization.

How Farming Got Started

How and why did humans begin to farm? We weren't there, so we can only speculate. Different scientists have various theories. Here are some.

- *Spilled-Grain Hypothesis*: Neolithic women—who probably gathered the wild grain—noticed that new grain plants grew when they accidentally spilled grain seeds. They tried scattering seeds on purpose, and it worked!

- *Watching-the-Animals Hypothesis*: Animals often find plants to eat in places with water and good soil. The people who hunted animals noticed this pattern. When people stayed at these sites, the animals became tamer. People started weeding and irrigating the plants so they would grow better. They also started saving the seeds of the better plants and planting them.

- *Moov'en-and-Groov'en Hypothesis*: One season, nomads liked a site so much they decided to stick around for a while. They stayed so long that they harvested a crop and then saw it grow to harvest stage again. These groups learned to grow a crop from seed to harvest and then move on.

Remember that a hypothesis is a theory or opinion that has not been proven—a kind of educated guess about what the evidence means.

Think For Yourself

1. Why was the introduction of farming such an important event in the story of human development?

2. On your own, explain why you agree with one of the hypotheses described above, or propose one of your own. Write down two facts or reasons to justify your hypothesis.

3. In a small group, discuss which hypothesis you think makes the most sense. Support your opinion with facts and reasons.

Testing a Hypothesis About Farming

The following article about the origins of farming was written by an historian at the Natural History Museum in England. The text of the article appears in black. Use the questions highlighted in red to help you think about how scientists justify hypotheses by finding supporting reasons and facts.

WHY FARMING BEGAN

The historian's hypothesis is stated in the first sentence. Do you agree with it? What support does the historian give for the hypothesis?

Farming probably developed in response to a shortage of food. Towards the end of the Ice Age, the human population was steadily increasing. But climatic changes had led to the extinction or migration of many of the larger animals. So, in many areas, there were far fewer animals to hunt. Also, in dry areas, people would be forced to live near permanent supplies of water.

What information does the historian add to support the argument?

We can imagine that the people in these settled communities must have been forced to store food for hard times. They probably stored nourishing grains and kept animals tethered as a kind of "walking food store." Such practices could have developed gradually into farming.

Using the legend, locate the places where scientists have found 7000-year-old evidence of early farming. Where are these sites located in relation to the equator? The Fertile Crescent was a vast region with the perfect climate for farming. For more information on this region, see Chapter 4.

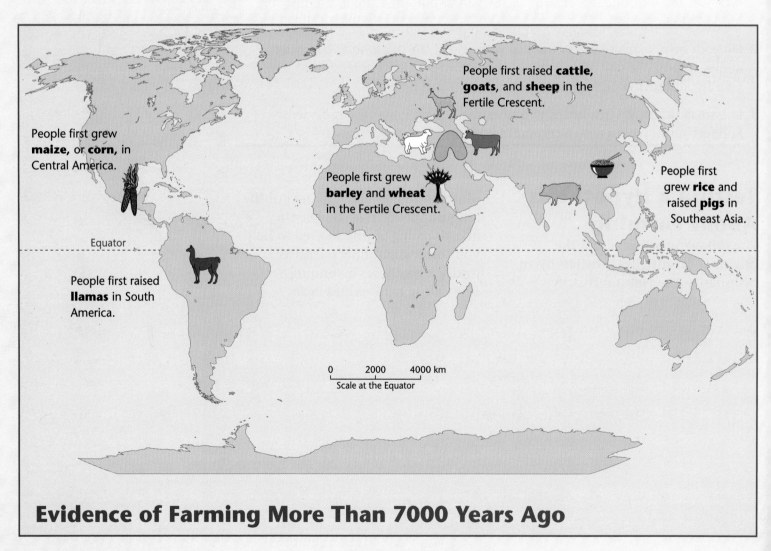

People first grew **maize,** or **corn,** in Central America.

People first raised **llamas** in South America.

People first raised **cattle, goats,** and **sheep** in the Fertile Crescent.

People first grew **barley** and **wheat** in the Fertile Crescent.

People first grew **rice** and raised **pigs** in Southeast Asia.

Equator

0   2000   4000 km
Scale at the Equator

Evidence of Farming More Than 7000 Years Ago

The fundamentals of farming haven't changed in 7000 years. It involves planting crops, harvesting crops, storing crops, herding animals, feeding animals, and breeding animals. What fundamentals are illustrated in these photographs?

How does planning help farmers avoid food shortages?

Farmers must be able to plan for the future. They must store grain for planting next year, and store food to feed themselves and their animals during the winter.

The historian's conclusion is in the first sentence in the following paragraph. How does the historian support the conclusion?

Farming was a very important step forward for modern humans because it was the solution to the problem of getting enough to eat. Farming produces more food from the same amount of land. So communities that adopted farming would have had an advantage over the hunters.

Their populations would have been able to increase. Many of these early farming settlements were the beginning of the towns and cities of the modern world.

Adapted from "The Development of Farming," Natural History Publications, *Man's Place in Evolution*, (London: The Natural History Museum, 1991), 86–91

A Closer Look

Farming in Jericho

Over 9000 years ago, 2000 people lived at Jericho [JAIR-ih-koh], a community near the Dead Sea. Hunting alone could not have supported such a large population, so archaeologists knew right away that these people must have been farmers. This excited the archaeologists, because Jericho was such an old site—it could be the place where farming began. The archaeologists began to unearth the evidence.

- *The excavators found grains of barley that were larger than barley grains that grow wild.*

- *They found small goat bones. The earliest tamed goats were often poorly fed, so they were small in size.*

- *They found flint **sickles**, a tool for cutting corn. Sickles are only useful for cutting a lot of corn—wild corn grows too scattered for a sickle to be useful.*

- *They found a grindstone, called a quern. Similar querns are used to grind corn in some communities even today.*

Here you can see a few of the sickle blades found in the ruins of ancient Jericho. The wooden handle has long since rotted away.

Try This

Meet with a partner to discuss how the historian argued a hypothesis in the article "Why Farming Began." Use the questions in the article to guide your discussion. Take turns reading the questions, and responding.

Think For Yourself

State your own hypothesis about how farming started. If you wrote one down before you read the article, use it. Then discuss the following with a partner.

- How is your hypothesis similar to and different from the one given in the article?

- Do you think the historian did a good job of supporting a hypothesis? Explain.

Ancient Mysteries

What Was Çatal Hüyük's Secret to Success?

Çatal Hüyük [CHAT-al HOO-yuk], in present-day Turkey, is one of the oldest cities ever found. Its ruins are over 8000 years old. The city has always puzzled archaeologists. They ask, for example, why were there no streets? You couldn't just stroll down the street in this city, because there were no streets at all. Through 800 years of city life, homes were built in clusters. Each house was built against the neighbours' houses. To visit a friend, you popped out of a hole in your roof, walked across the roofs of your neighbours, and then disappeared through a hole

into your friend's home. Why did the people of Çatal Hüyük build their homes this way? No one knows.

We do know about 5000 people lived together in these flat apartment buildings. What inspired these people to live together? We can only assume that life was better together than it was apart. The city bustled with activity. Excavators have found evidence of craft making and trade. Wall paintings, jewellery, cosmetics, cloth, and statues—and the oldest mirror in the world—have all appeared in

the ruins. Farming seems to have been easy in Çatal Hüyük. A nearby river brought fertile soil and water for crops. Over time, the people became experts at raising food and animals, including dogs and sheep.

The people of Çatal Hüyük had few natural resources besides food, reeds, and clay. Yet they created a society that brought a good standard of living to 5000 people. What was their secret? Perhaps living so close together, they learned to co-operate. We'll never know for sure.

Cities: Another Giant Step

Besides a chance to make a living, the walled city offered safety—large numbers of people that live close together can protect themselves more easily from enemies.

Looking at how cities have developed is like seeing civilization evolve. First, the development of farming brought people together in communities. When the farmlands produced more food than the farmers needed to feed their families, some people stopped farming. They developed other skills and moved closer together, forming villages.

Sometimes these villages grew into towns, and then cities.

Ancient Cities of the World

In ancient times, cities were the homes of royalty and the officials who held power. These officials

Here are the ruins of Great Zimbabwe, the royal city of ancient Zimbabwe. Here the royal family lived in a huge stone structure. How would such a home affect the status of the ancient kings?

usually controlled the surrounding land and decided who could farm it. Some cities grew up around a temple or other place of worship. These communities flourished because people found they could make a living in the town as shopkeepers, craftspeople, artists, teachers, priests, and officials.

Scientists love to discover the ruins of ancient cities. They want to know how ancient people lived and met their individual and common needs.

Seeing Patterns

When we look at the development of different early civilizations, we can see a pattern to the changes. From nomadic groups travelling in search of food, people formed settled, organized communities. These communities grew into cities and eventually met other groups through trade or warfare. Cities developed unique characteristics and solved their problems in different ways. Most of them, however, developed through all the stages shown in the picture series on the next page.

These deserted ruins reveal Tulum, an ancient Mayan city on the Yucatan Peninsula in Mexico. How would the city's seaside location have benefited the people?

Viewing Hint

Before you read the text and view the pictures on the next page, try a little game: Identify the different stages of community development by examining the pictures.

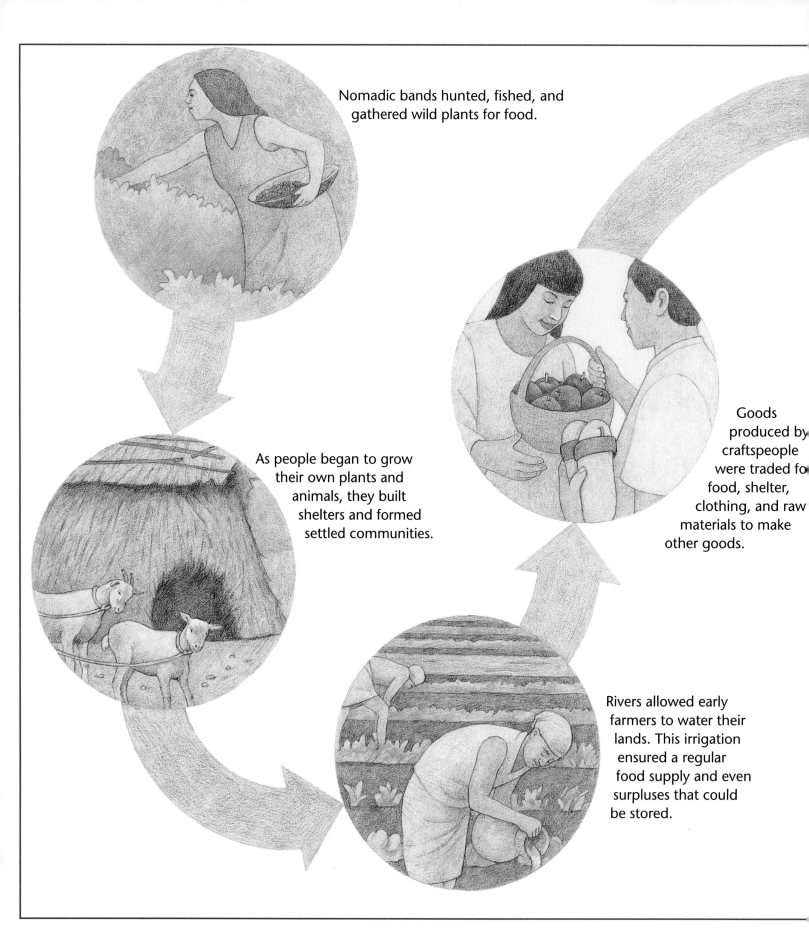

Nomadic bands hunted, fished, and gathered wild plants for food.

As people began to grow their own plants and animals, they built shelters and formed settled communities.

Rivers allowed early farmers to water their lands. This irrigation ensured a regular food supply and even surpluses that could be stored.

Goods produced by craftspeople were traded for food, shelter, clothing, and raw materials to make other goods.

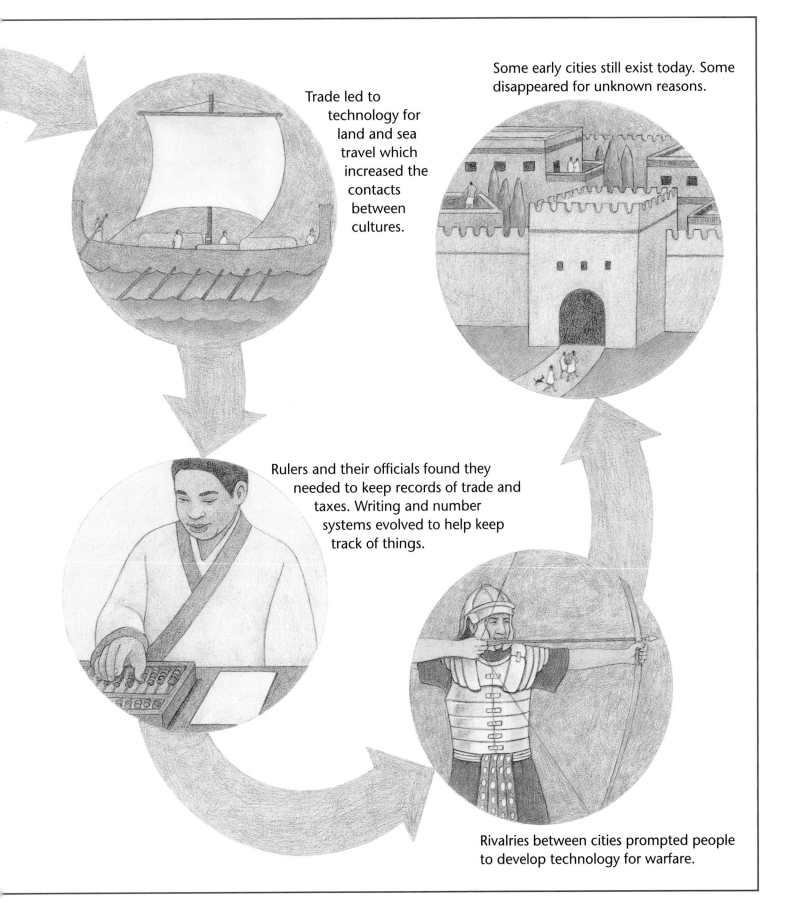

Trade led to technology for land and sea travel which increased the contacts between cultures.

Some early cities still exist today. Some disappeared for unknown reasons.

Rulers and their officials found they needed to keep records of trade and taxes. Writing and number systems evolved to help keep track of things.

Rivalries between cities prompted people to develop technology for warfare.

Try This

1. Examine the information in the picture series on pages 62–63. Make a two-column chart. In the first column, list all the stages—or changes—you see, in order. In the second column, speculate on how each change must have affected people's lives.

2. With a partner, discuss how the events described in the chart did or did not contribute to a more civilized life for people.

3. In your opinion, which was the most important step in getting civilization started: invention of fire, tools for hunting, the beginning of farming, technology for travel, or the beginning of cities? Remember to support your opinion.

Looking Back

In this chapter, you've examined the big steps that led towards civilization. You have seen that tools played a crucial role at every step. What tool do you think had the greatest effect?

Chapter 4

Mesopotamia: Cradle of Civilization

Where would *you* build a city? In what kind of place could a lot of people live together, get the food they need, and do all the activities that always go on in cities?

If you visited the land where the world's first cities appeared, you might be surprised. You'd find a hot, dry place—almost a desert. Only a few trees dot the landscape, and you wouldn't see any stone or other building materials.

About five thousand years ago, an ancient farming people turned this harsh environment into an abundant garden. Their agricultural settlements grew into the world's first great cities. And within these cities, the world's first civilization burst into life. We call the land of this incredible people *Mesopotamia* [me-suh-puh-TAY-mee-uh].

In this chapter, you will see how the environment of Mesopotamia helped civilization flourish. You'll see how contact with other peoples benefited Mesopotamians but also brought conflict to the land.

Land Between Rivers

Farming technology consists of the tools we make and use to grow food.

The Fertile Crescent was an arc of land in the Middle East that had good soil, a hot climate, and water.

Civilization develops only when people have plenty of food, and only farmers can produce plenty of food. The people who settled in Mesopotamia took full advantage of a fertile land and hot climate by developing their farming methods and **farming technology**. They created an abundance of food never seen before.

A Fertile Valley

Mesopotamia was part of the area known as the **Fertile Crescent**. This arc of land stretched from the northern end of the Persian Gulf to the Nile River valley in Egypt. The Fertile Crescent was an ideal place for farming. Along the rivers, the land was rich in edible plants, especially fruit, wheat, and barley. Fish and birds were plentiful. Pigs, sheep, and goats lived in the wild. Over time, people learned to **domesticate** [duh-MES-TIH-kate], or tame, the animals and wild plants so that they would have a steady supply of food.

The Tigris and the Euphrates Rivers begin in the mountains of Turkey. Water rushes down to the hills below, picking up fertile silt and carrying it to the valley floor. What other river valley do you know of that has good farmland?

Mesopotamia is the ancient name for the **plain**, or large flat area that stretches between the Tigris [TY-gris] River on the east and the Euphrates [yoo-FRAY-tees] River on the west. These rivers begin in mountains to the north and flow through the valley towards the Persian Gulf. In ancient times, the **silt** (fine sand) carried downstream by the rivers built up along the riverbeds, creating excellent, fertile soil.

Near the gulf, the rivers split into smaller streams, creating a marshy area called a **delta**. Besides attracting plenty of wildlife for hunting and fishing, the marshy swamps provided reeds that made excellent materials for building houses.

The name "Mesopotamia," which comes to us from Greek, means "the land between two rivers."

When we speak of Mesopotamian civilization, we really mean the four civilizations that existed on the Mesopotamian plain: Sumer [SOOM-ur], Babylon [BAB-ih-lon], Assyria [uh-SEER-ee-uh], and Chaldea [kal-DEE-uh]. Find these civilizations on the map and identify the date when each began. What pattern do you see?

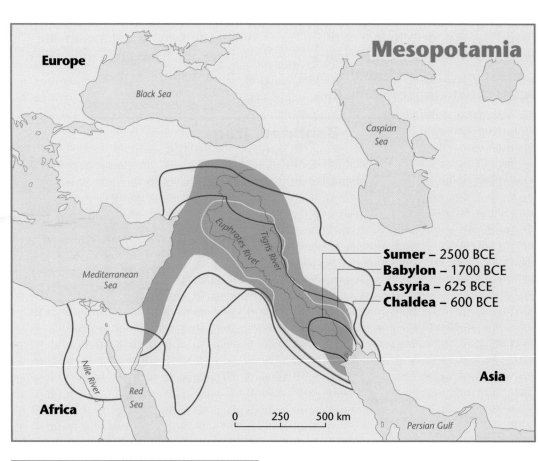

Mesopotamia

Sumer – 2500 BCE
Babylon – 1700 BCE
Assyria – 625 BCE
Chaldea – 600 BCE

This map shows the modern political boundaries of the area shown in the map above. Most of Mesopotamia lay in the area we now know as Iraq [ih-RAK].

Investigate

All over the world, cities have flourished along river valleys. In an atlas, find 10 of the world's largest cities. How many of these cities are located beside a river? What conclusion can you make?

A Hot, Dry Climate

The early farmers of Mesopotamia found the hot, dry climate of the region to be both a blessing and a curse. It provided the heat that many plants need to thrive but not the rainfall. In spring, fields flooded after the snow melted in the mountains. When the water was gone, in late summer, the fields and crops baked in the hot sun.

This **climagraph** [KLY-muh-graf] shows the average monthly temperatures and rainfall for Baghdad [BAG-dad], Iraq. Many scientists believe that the climate of Baghdad is just like Mesopotamia's was 5000 years ago. The annual **precipitation** [prih-sip-uh-TAY-shun] of Vancouver is 1167 mm. How does this compare with Baghdad's?

Precipitation can be rain, snow, or hail.

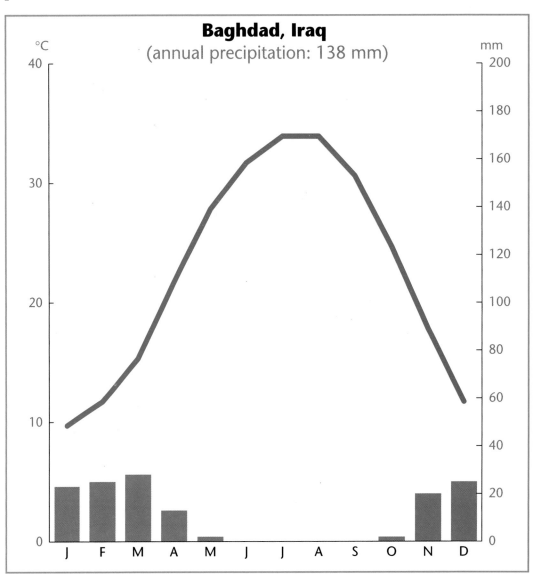

Baghdad, Iraq
(annual precipitation: 138 mm)

HOW TO... Make a Climagraph

The two pieces of information that tell us the most about the climate of a region are its precipitation and temperature patterns. By looking at both pieces of information together, we can see what the weather will be like at any time of year.

The table below shows the average monthly precipitation and temperature for Vancouver, BC. Follow the steps below to make a climagraph of Vancouver.

	Temperature (°C)	Precipitation (mm)
January	3.0	150
February	4.7	124
March	6.3	109
April	8.8	75
May	12.1	62
June	15.2	46
July	17.2	36
August	17.4	38
September	14.3	64
October	10.0	115
November	6.0	170
December	3.5	178
Annual		1167

This table shows the temperature and precipitation for Vancouver, British Columbia. After you have made your climagraph, decide which form of presentation—table or climagraph—makes the information easiest to understand.

1. Start by making a graph like the one for Baghdad. Label the twelve months across the bottom. Label the temperature units along the left side in red. Label the precipitation units in blue along the right. Write the annual precipitation at the top.

2. Make a dot in the first column, to show the temperature for January. Mark the temperature for each month the same way. Connect the dots with a red line.

3. In the first column, use a ruler to draw a line showing the total precipitation for January. Do the same for every month. Fill in every bar with blue.

Throughout history, people have settled along river systems because these areas have such rich soil. Unfortunately, this also puts them in the **flood plain**—the area of land that floods when the river overflows its banks.

Try This

1. Compare the temperatures and precipitation of Baghdad and Vancouver. What differences do you notice between the two climates? How are these two climates similar to and different from the climate where you live? Make a climagraph for your community to help you answer this question.

2. What characteristics of the environment and landscape of Mesopotamia made it suitable for the development of a civilization? What factors of the environment and landscape worked against the people?

You may want to make a chart like this one to help organize your thinking.

Suitable for development	Unsuitable for development

After people learned to build dams and irrigation systems such as the Assyrian method shown below, they could control the spring floods. This made the flood plain a much safer place to live and farm. Why was a stone attached to the pole?

Adapting the Environment

Except for springtime floods, Mesopotamia was a dry land. After the floodwaters flowed away, the people were left with sun-baked ground. The biggest challenge for the farmers was to control the flow of water so that the fields would neither flood nor bake. Only in this way could they make sure their crops would survive.

The people found ways to **irrigate** [IR-uh-gate] the land, or bring water to their fields. At first, people dug away parts of the riverbank so that the water would flood onto their land. They built dams to make pools and dipped water out of them with buckets tied to poles. They built **dikes** (a low earthen wall) to direct the flow of water. Later, they created a complex network of irrigation ditches and canals. This irrigation system forced people to work together because they had to maintain the canals for the good of everyone.

People have used dams for many purposes. This dam was owned by a Canadian mining company. It once held back poisonous waste from a mine in Spain. When the dam broke, the waste poured onto nearby farmland.

The network of canals brought greater communication and co-operation among towns, as well. The canals and rivers became the roadways of the Mesopotamians.

As it turned out, the methods used by the Mesopotamians created an even more difficult problem. Because of the farmers' success, food grew plentifully. The population increased, and so did the need for water. The desert soil contained a lot of salt, however. The irrigation caused this salt to rise to the surface of the soil. The extra salt poisoned the plants. The more the people irrigated their fields with water from the rivers, the saltier the soil became. After a few hundred years of irrigation, the soil could no longer produce crops. The people of these cities either died off or moved to more fertile land. New cities would arise at the new location.

Trace the series of causes and effects that, in turn, brought to an end the powerful cities of Sumer, Babylon, Assyria, and Chaldea. Do you think it's possible to predict long-term consequences and avoid them? Why or why not?

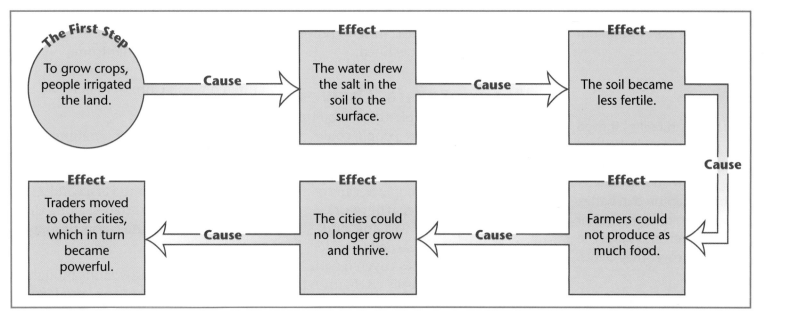

The First Step
To grow crops, people irrigated the land.

— Cause → **Effect** The water drew the salt in the soil to the surface.

— Cause → **Effect** The soil became less fertile.

Cause

Effect Traders moved to other cities, which in turn became powerful.

← Cause — **Effect** The cities could no longer grow and thrive.

← Cause — **Effect** Farmers could not produce as much food.

Think For Yourself

By irrigating the land, the people of Mesopotamia made the land too salty to produce food. It is easy to look back in time to make judgments about others' mistakes. But what about us today? Are we having some impacts on our environment that could cause problems in the future? Think about the following actions of people:

- A family buys a second car.
- A student makes a lunch that includes a disposable plastic container.

In a two-column chart, list at least one consequence for each action. Then add three more actions and consequences.

Contact and Conflict

Mesopotamian women enjoyed several freedoms. They could own property and slaves, run businesses, and take part in trading.

The communities thrived partly through the hard work of slaves. Some people were made slaves after being captured in battle. Others sold themselves or their children into slavery to cover their debts.

A community's economy is its wealth and resources.

Like the history of all civilizations, Mesopotamia's history can be described as a series of contacts and conflicts. Each of the four major civilizations—Sumer, Babylon, Assyria, and Chaldea—rose to power, thrived, and then declined.

Mesopotamia Thrives

Because there was plenty of food in Mesopotamia, some people could make a living by creating goods or selling their services in exchange for surplus food. People began to develop skills in leatherwork, pottery, carpentry, weaving, and metalwork. They learned to make gold rings, statuettes covered with **lapis lazuli** [LAH-pis LAH-zuh-ly] (a blue gemstone), and shell containers for make-up. By trading these goods, people could make a good living—the **economy** thrived.

With its many rivers and canals, the region soon became a centre of trade. The Sumerian traders sailed up and down the Tigris and Euphrates Rivers in small boats made of reeds with goatskin sails. They also traded with their neighbours throughout the Mediterranean. Caravans and long ships powered by square sails and oars carried building stone from Africa, copper from Cyprus, gold from Egypt, and cedar from Lebanon. In trade, the Sumerians offered wool, cloth, jewellery, oil, and grains.

Babylon thrived as a trading centre because it lay at the centre of the main trade routes. Babylonian caravans travelled to Persia and Asia Minor. Their ships traded along the rivers and along the coasts of Arabia and India.

Trade with nearby lands brought more than goods. People also learned about one another's language, religion, and inventions. For example, new ways of making pottery and new tools for farming spread quickly through the Mediterranean after they appeared in Mesopotamia. This "trade" in ideas helped the Mesopotamian society flourish.

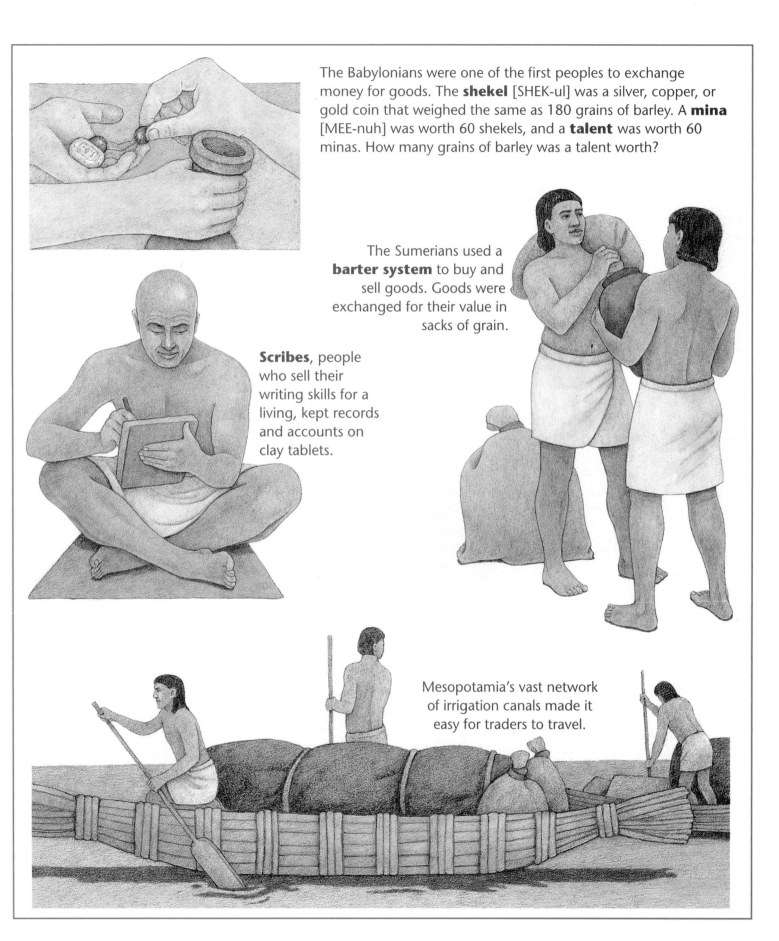

The Babylonians were one of the first peoples to exchange money for goods. The **shekel** [SHEK-ul] was a silver, copper, or gold coin that weighed the same as 180 grains of barley. A **mina** [MEE-nuh] was worth 60 shekels, and a **talent** was worth 60 minas. How many grains of barley was a talent worth?

The Sumerians used a **barter system** to buy and sell goods. Goods were exchanged for their value in sacks of grain.

Scribes, people who sell their writing skills for a living, kept records and accounts on clay tablets.

Mesopotamia's vast network of irrigation canals made it easy for traders to travel.

The peoples of Mesopotamia traded goods with people throughout their corner of the world. Did Sumerians trade their goods for raw materials or finished goods? Why?

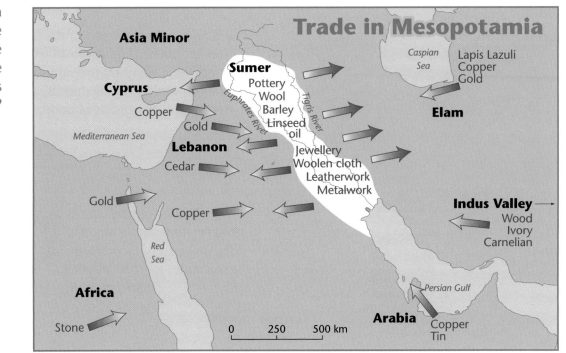

Trade in Mesopotamia

Asia Minor

Cyprus
Copper

Mediterranean Sea

Sumer
Pottery
Wool
Barley
Linseed oil

Lebanon
Cedar

Gold

Gold

Copper

Red Sea

Africa

Stone

Caspian Sea

Lapis Lazuli
Copper
Gold

Elam

Jewellery
Woolen cloth
Leatherwork
Metalwork

Indus Valley
Wood
Ivory
Carnelian

Persian Gulf

Arabia
Copper
Tin

0   250   500 km

Ancient Stories

Voyage to Nippur

The Mesopotamians were the first people to leave a written record of their civilization. Thousands of clay tablets tell us about their daily lives. By piecing together the fragments of information, we have gradually come to understand what life was like in Mesopotamia. One writer, Elizabeth Lansing, used this knowledge to create a fictional account of the journey of a Sumerian trader from his home city of Erech along the Euphrates River to another Sumerian city, Nippur [NIP-poor]. As you read, you'll notice that the trader seems to be gathering information. Think about why he might be doing so.

The riverbanks were wide bands of green, dotted with date palms and thick patches of reeds. Near the half dozen cities that lay between Erech and Nippur the belts of green broadened out into cultivated fields and pastureland, vineyards, and groves of fig trees. These lands were the property of each walled city. Their size and state of cultivation were an indication of the city's prosperity.

The river itself was a lively place, for the muddy waters of the Euphrates provided the broad highway between one Sumerian city and another. Many of the craft were long trading vessels, such as the one in which the man from Erech journeyed. Among them were vessels capable of travelling long distances. Sometimes, aided by a huge square-shaped sail, they ventured far out on the wide waters of the Mediterranean Sea to the west to bring cedars from Lebanon or stone and precious metals from the lands to the north. Smaller basket-like boats were more common. They crowded the waters, particularly near the wharves of each walled city….

In the fields and vineyards surrounding the walled cities that he passed, workers were gathering in the harvest…. Both men and beasts were taking the harvest to the temple compound within the city. There the harvest would be **allotted** [divided into shares] and distributed to the people….

The stranger's boat was approaching Nippur. The high walls of Sumer's cultural city rose splendidly above the broad fields that stretched away for miles on either side of the river…. The traffic thickened as the long, high-decked boat drew nearer to Nippur….

The logs of cedar heaped along the wharf told [the trader] that Nippur was trading with the northern provinces, where the trees grew in the great forest of the mountains. The bars of gold and copper were evidence that Nippur was in touch with the lands to the east. He took careful note of these signs of prosperity. Later he would hire a scribe to write his observations with a **stylus** [reed pen] on a soft bit of clay. He himself could not write; that was an art for the learned men and was perhaps beneath his dignity as a member of his king's household.

Once beyond the dock area, the stranger followed a hard-packed dirt roadway leading toward the Nanna Gate…. Like the wharf area, it swarmed with activity. A cloud of dust rose above the laden donkeys; herds of sheep and goats were being pushed and prodded along in the direction of the gate. Wheeled carts, heaped with goods and produce, rattled past, drawn by oxen or pairs of donkeys. The crowd grew thicker as the massive gate loomed closer.

A shouted order sent the entire throng scurrying back. A two-wheeled military chariot drawn by four donkeys swept out from the city. A driver, wearing a bronze helmet, stood on the axle, supporting himself by gripping a fleece-covered headboard. He guided the donkeys with long leather reins fixed to their noses by a ring. After the chariot, marching four abreast and wearing leather tunics, came a detachment of foot soldiers. Their highly polished short swords and shields gleamed in the sun. This was a guard detail, one of the many that watched over the city. The stranger, from his place in the shadow of the gate, observed that the soldiers looked tough and hardy, a fact that would interest his king.

From Elizabeth Lansing, "A Stranger in Nippur," *The Sumerians: Inventors and Builders*, (Toronto: McGraw-Hill Book Company, 1971), 54–61

The trader scurries out of the way to avoid being trampled by the military chariot coming through the Nanna Gate.

Try This

1. Look back through "Voyage to Nippur" to find out what the trader found interesting. Put the following items in the first column of a two-column chart. Add your own findings. Then, in the second column, describe what each discovery told the trader about Nippur.

   What the Trader Saw

   • pastureland, vineyards, and groves of fig trees

   • vessels in the harbour that could travel long distances

   • cedar logs heaped along the wharf

   • bars of gold and copper

   • a wharf area busy with people moving goods and animals towards the city

   • people moving out of the way quickly when a military chariot arrives

2. Think, pair, share. Think about the following question and write down your thoughts. "What made Nippur a good place for people to build a city?" Discuss your ideas with a partner. Then, with your partner, meet with another pair of students to share your ideas.

Conflict and Warfare

Competition for the growing wealth of the Fertile Crescent brought conflict.

As you saw previously, trade and other peaceful contact enriched the civilization of Mesopotamia. But other contact led to warfare. When a civilization traded regularly with its neighbours, it usually flourished. But if it had many strong enemies, it was usually doomed.

The battleship *Missouri* fires its guns during the Gulf War, a war fought in the Middle East near the former lands of Mesopotamia. As in the battle pictured on the clay tablet shown on the next page, this war was a fight over land and resources. Compare the technologies of war shown in these two pictures.

How was conflict a part of life in Mesopotamia? We could use many types of information to find out. Three that help us discover the stories of the ancient world are artifacts, chronologies, and maps.

Artifacts Help Tell the Story

Look at the following artifacts to learn more about conflict in Mesopotamia. What special kinds of information do you learn by studying pictures of artifacts and their captions?

This **relief** (carving on a stone surface) was found at the palace of Ashurbanipal at Niniveh [NIN-uh-vuh]. Each soldier has a different task. What are they?

This artifact shows Babylonian battle techniques.

This artifact shows that war prisoners were treated harshly.

This relief, found in the palace of Ashurnazirpal II in Nimrud [NIM-rood], shows an Assyrian soldier killing a captive. Some captives were killed; others became slaves or labourers.

This artifact shows scenes of war (on the back of the panel) and celebration together.

The Standard of Ur [UR] (made about 2700 BCE) was probably the sounding board of a **lyre**, a mini harp. This inlay of shell and lapis lazuli shows a banquet with animals and men carrying goods. The other side of the standard shows a scene of war. Why would a banquet and a war be shown together?

Chronologies Help Tell the Story

Chronologies [kruh-NOL-uh-jeez] list important events or developments over a period of time. They always list the events in order, from earliest to most recent. Some chronologies are set up as time lines, which help us see the events spaced out in relation to one another. As you read the following chronology, think about its strengths and weaknesses as a source of information.

A Chronology of Mesopotamian Empires

6000 BCE Early herders and farmers from the north move into the Tigris and Euphrates River valleys, farming villages and towns. They begin raising animals, growing crops, and irrigating fields. In times of severe drought, herders who live on the edge of the desert move into the cultivated areas and allow their herds to feed on the crops in the fields. This usually leads to conflict.

3500 BCE The use of irrigation ensures a food supply for the growing cities. Artisans and merchants living in the cities help trade expand. Cities give rise to the Sumerian civilization.

3000 BCE Under the rule of the first kings, cities become **city-states**. A city-state is independent and does not belong to a country. Trade grows with cultures in Anatolia [a-nuh-TOLE-ee-uh], Syria [SEER-ee-uh], Persia [PUR-zhuh], and the Indus [IN-dus] Valley. Conflict among the city-states over water and land lead to a constant state of warfare.

2300 BCE The Akkadians [uh-KAY-dee-uns] overpower the Sumerians, uniting the whole region into the first Mesopotamian Empire. A short period of peace follows.

2125 BCE The Sumerians revive and conquer the region. Art and writing flourish, and some of the great structures are built.

1792–1595 BCE Under Hammurabi [ham-uh-RAH-bee], Babylon gains control. The economy thrives throughout Mesopotamia. Astronomy and the arts flourish before Babylon is conquered by the Hittites [HIT-tites].

1595–1157 BCE A chaotic age lasts for centuries. Several empires rise and fall, but none can create a lasting empire because tribes on the edges of Mesopotamia continue to attack.

883–612 BCE With chariots and iron weapons, Assyria rises to a position of power over the region, ruling its neighbours as far away as Egypt.

612–539 BCE The Chaldeans defeat the Assyrians. A new Babylonian empire emerges. Nebuchadnezzar [neb-uh-kud-NEZ-ur] brings Babylon new glory and takes the Israelites captive.

539 BCE–CE 637 Eleven centuries of foreign rule begin with the Persian capture of Babylon in 590 BCE.

Maps Help Tell the Story

Maps can help us understand the history of an area. For example, we can see how political boundaries change over time, or how an area's landforms make it vulnerable to invasion. We can also use maps to present specialized information such as the location of natural resources or settlements. As you examine the map below, think about the strengths and limitations of the information in maps.

This city map shows the major features of Nippur, the sacred city of Sumer. It is based on a map of the city created about 1300 BCE. Find the Nanna Gate, which is the gate used by the fictional trader in the Ancient Stories feature on pages 74–75.

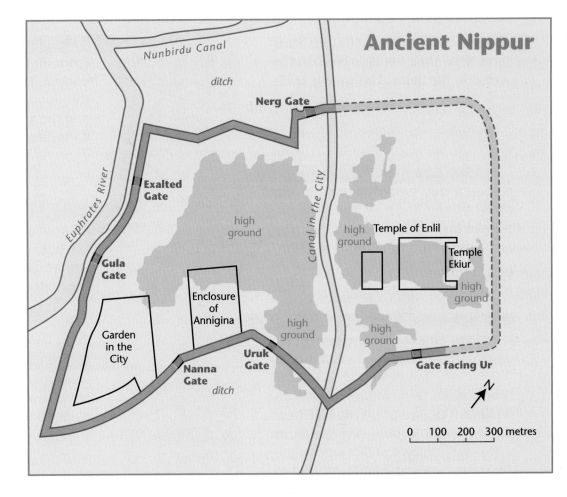

Ancient Nippur

Nunbirdu Canal

ditch

Nerg Gate

Exalted Gate

Euphrates River

Canal in the City

high ground

high ground

Temple of Enlil

Temple Ekiur

high ground

Gula Gate

Enclosure of Annigina

high ground

high ground

Garden in the City

Nanna Gate

ditch

Uruk Gate

Gate facing Ur

0   100   200   300 metres

Try This

1. Think, pair, share. Think about the following question and write down your thoughts. "In what ways was contact both good and bad for Mesopotamia?" Discuss your ideas with a partner. Then, with your partner, meet with another pair of students to share your ideas.

2. Work with a partner to create a chart showing the strengths and limitations of the three sources of information described in this section: artifacts, chronologies, and maps.

Innovations of Mesopotamia

Can you imagine life without the wheel? How about books or laws? You wouldn't have to go to school, but you couldn't do much else that you're used to. Depending on where you live, you and your family might end up living a simple lifestyle, hauling heavy loads of fuel and water on your back, growing vegetables on a small plot of land, and living in fear of attack by hungry neighbours.

The Mesopotamians were the first to discover or invent some of the most basic improvements in human life. Their **innovations**—or new ways of doing things—changed the way people lived in much of the world. Just consider the most famous of these innovations: the wheel, sailing ships, writing, irrigation, law, and **architecture** [AR-kuh-tek-chur].

Engineering

Although we can only guess how the wheel was discovered, the Mesopotamians were the first humans to use it. The wheel changed human life greatly. It allowed people to build wagons to transport goods and to build war chariots. Wheels were also used as pulleys to raise water from wells. Using potter's wheels, potters could make fine pottery.

How has the wheel made life easier for the woman on the right?

Farming Technology

The people of Mesopotamia invented many tools and techniques to make their farming work easier and more productive. They harnessed animals to pull ploughs. They placed a shoulder yoke on oxen to make them easier to guide. They altered the plough so that it would turn the soil and drop seeds into the freshly ploughed rows.

Architecture is the art of designing buildings.

Astronomy

Mesopotamian **astronomers** worked out a twelve-month calendar based on the cycles of the moon. They divided the year into two seasons: summer and winter.

An astronomer [uh-STRON-uh-mur] is someone who studies the universe.

Mathematics

The Mesopotamians used mathematics to build canals, to keep accurate farm and trade records, and to calculate the taxes each family owed to the state. Their counting system was based on the number 60. We still use 60 when we measure the degrees in a circle or count time in minutes and seconds.

Writing

The Mesopotamians were the first people to develop written language. Writing was probably first used to keep track of trade. Education, laws, history, and literature all became possible after humans could record their ideas. The Sumerians developed a form of writing called "cuneiform."

A Closer Look

Cuneiform

The Sumerians developed the earliest known system of writing, called cuneiform [kyoo-NAY-uh-form]. Cuneiform first appeared in Sumer about 3000 BCE. It evolved from simple picture signs for words, called **pictographs** [PIK-tuh-grafs]. At first, one pictograph was marked on one small clay token, to symbolize and record a trade. Then someone realized it was handier to mark several pictographs on one large clay tablet. Pictographs evolved over the years into symbols that stood for sounds instead of words. The name cuneiform means "wedge-shaped" from the shape of the marks made by the reed pens used to write on clay tablets.

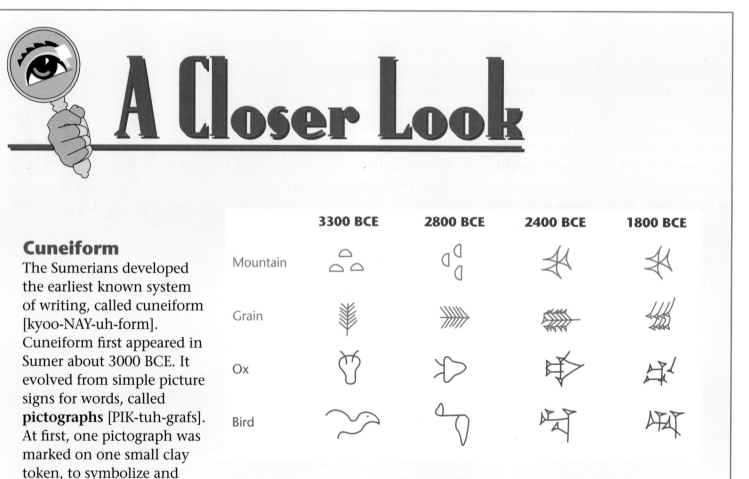

	3300 BCE	2800 BCE	2400 BCE	1800 BCE
Mountain				
Grain				
Ox				
Bird				

After people get used to writing, they tend to write faster. Over time, the early pictographs were simplified into strokes that could be written more quickly. Would this make learning to write easier or more difficult?

Think For Yourself

What did the people of Mesopotamia use writing for? How do you think the invention might have developed? How do you think this invention changed people's lives? What would life be like today without writing?

Laws

With the development of writing, the Mesopotamians began to write down laws. The best-known set of laws of the ancient Mesopotamians is the Code of Hammurabi. Hammurabi was a king of Babylon. He brought prosperity and peace to the city-states he ruled throughout Mesopotamia. He claimed that the gods had told him to write down laws to make sure that "the strong may not oppress the weak." This set of laws helps us understand the values and customs of the ancient Babylonians.

Hammurabi's code was an important step toward creating a society in which everyone's rights are recognized. The code lists 282 laws. They cover all aspects of people's daily life, including family, labour, buying and selling land, possessions, and trade. Each law has a set punishment.

All civilizations have laws that say what people can and cannot do. When laws are written down, everyone knows them and everyone can expect equal treatment. Why do you think laws are considered a sign of civilization?

Hammurabi's complete code of laws was carved onto this stela [STEEL-uh], an upright stone. The stela originally stood in a temple in Babylon. More recently, it was moved to a museum in Paris, France. Do you think this is a good place to keep the stela? Why, or why not?

PERSPECTIVES

Hammurabi vs. Canadian Law

Hammurabi's laws were based on the idea of "an eye for an eye." People could be put to death, lose an eye or a limb, be tortured, or have their children put to death, sometimes for minor crimes. It was believed that tough punishments would scare people into obeying the law. Decide if the following sample laws would stop you from disobeying the law.

- If a noble destroys the eye of another noble, his eye shall be destroyed.

- If a noble destroys the eye of a commoner or breaks the bone of a commoner, he shall pay one mina of silver.

- If a noble destroys the eye of a noble's slave, he shall pay one-half the slave's value.

- If a man helps a male or female slave escape through the city gates, he shall be put to death.

- If a house collapses causing the death of a son of the owner of the house, the son of the builder of the house shall be put to death.

- If a son strikes his father, his hand shall be cut off.

- If [a woman] has not been discreet, has gone out, ruined her house, belittled her husband, she shall be drowned.

In Canada, we believe that people will obey the law out of respect rather than fear. We believe that people who break the law can learn from their mistakes and should be given a second chance. Our laws are also meant to protect people from being punished for something they did not do.

Consider the first of Hammurabi's laws in the list above. In Canada, if someone caused another person to lose an eye, the punishment would depend on a lot of things. For example, here are some of the questions that we would ask in a Canadian court of law.

- Is the offender a youth or an adult?

- Was the crime committed on purpose?

- Has the offender caused similar injuries before?

- Does the offender admit guilt?

- Is the offender likely to commit the crime again?

- Should the offender be treated less harshly for some reason (e.g., fatal illness)?

- Is the offender sorry?

Different answers to these questions would lead to different punishments. Do you think Canada's or Hammurabi's laws are better? Why?

Think For Yourself

List six ways our lives would be different without the innovations mentioned in this section. Which of the innovations of the Mesopotamians do you think was the most important to future people? Give at least two examples showing how that invention or innovation changed peoples' lives. Be prepared to present your opinion to the class.

Try This

Mesopotamia was fortunate in many ways and unfortunate in others. For example:

Fortunately, Mesopotamia had lots of food.	Unfortunately, lots of people wanted it.
Fortunately, the landforms of Mesopotamia made travel easy.	Unfortunately, the landforms made Mesopotamia easy to attack.

Create some more "Fortunately/Unfortunately" statements about Mesopotamia.

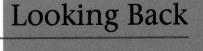

Looking Back

In this chapter you have seen the beginnings of civilization. You saw how the environment encouraged the development of cities, and how contact with other peoples brought both benefits and drawbacks to Mesopotamia. What do you think was the most important factor that made civilization possible in Mesopotamia?

Chapter 5

Egypt: Gift of the Nile

L et's say you're preparing a time capsule to show people 5000 years from now what our civilization was like. What kinds of things would you choose to present our best accomplishments? What artifacts would show future people how we lived?

The undisturbed tombs of the ancient Egyptians, discovered deep within the great pyramids, are like gigantic, 5000-year-old time capsules. When archaeologists discovered them, they opened a window on the past. The tombs were filled with writings, wall paintings, and treasures—as well as mummified bodies and containers of food and wine. From all this evidence, archaeologists have been able to see into Egypt's incredible past.

In this chapter, you can learn about the features that all civilizations share, including ancient Egypt. You can also examine a feature of Egyptian civilization that interests you most.

Civilization on the Nile

For the ancient Egyptians, one event came like a gift each year: the moment when the Nile River flooded its banks and covered the land. As the river waters gradually drained away, they left behind a layer of rich **silt** (fine, fertile soil) that turned the desert beside the river into green fields. With the abundant food the yearly floods made possible, the early settlements of hunter-gatherers developed into a complex culture that lasted thousands of years.

Ancient Egypt was a very hot, very dry land. Temperatures could reach 50°C. The only major source of water was the Nile River. From the Nile's origins, deep in central Africa, the river flowed northward. Ribbons of green hugged the sides of the river, cutting through the Sahara Desert. Over a thousand kilometres north, the river divided and divided again into a **delta**—a triangle-shaped marshy area on the north coast of Africa. Here the river waters finally met the salt waters of the Mediterranean Sea.

Each spring, heavy rains and melted snow from central Africa rushed down the river. All along the Nile Valley, the river flooded its banks, soaking the land. As the floodwaters went down, they left behind a fringe of fertile black soil. Because the water drained, and did not evaporate, it left behind few of the harmful salts that poisoned the land of Mesopotamia.

A Greek historian who visited Egypt around 500 BCE noticed how important the Nile was to life. He described the civilization of ancient Egypt as "the gift of the Nile."

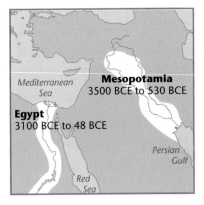

Before the Nile emptied into the Mediterranean Sea, the river waters made their way through a marshy river delta. Here you can see the Nile Delta as it looks from space.

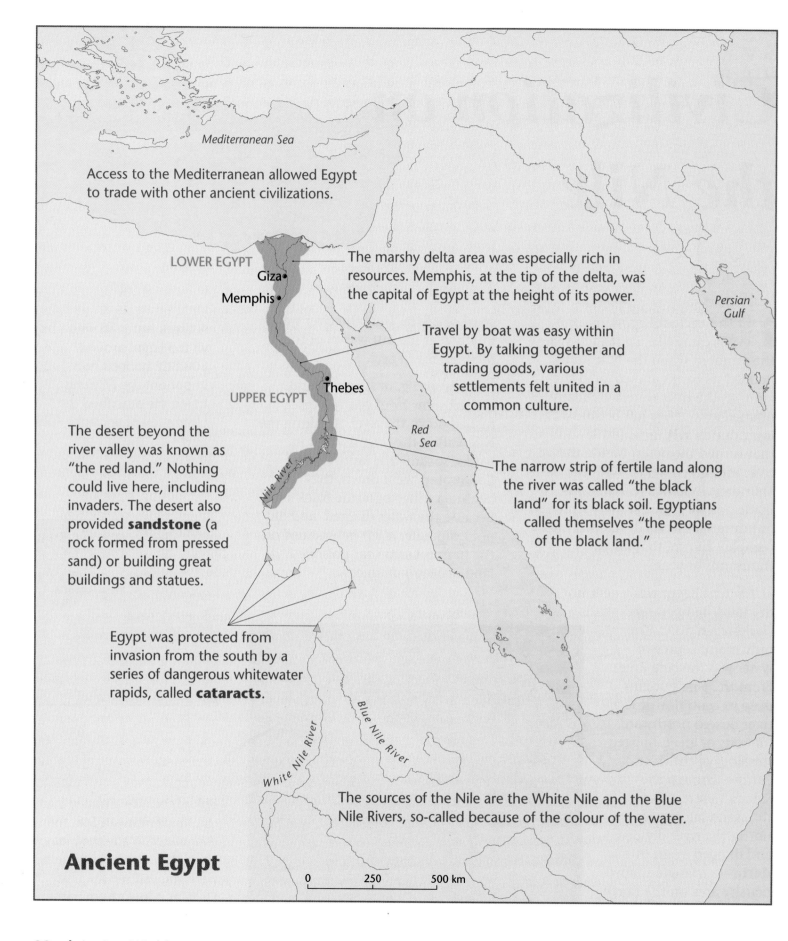

Access to the Mediterranean allowed Egypt to trade with other ancient civilizations.

The marshy delta area was especially rich in resources. Memphis, at the tip of the delta, was the capital of Egypt at the height of its power.

Travel by boat was easy within Egypt. By talking together and trading goods, various settlements felt united in a common culture.

The desert beyond the river valley was known as "the red land." Nothing could live here, including invaders. The desert also provided **sandstone** (a rock formed from pressed sand) or building great buildings and statues.

The narrow strip of fertile land along the river was called "the black land" for its black soil. Egyptians called themselves "the people of the black land."

Egypt was protected from invasion from the south by a series of dangerous whitewater rapids, called **cataracts**.

The sources of the Nile are the White Nile and the Blue Nile Rivers, so-called because of the colour of the water.

Mediterranean Sea

LOWER EGYPT

Giza

Memphis

UPPER EGYPT

Thebes

Red Sea

Persian Gulf

Nile River

White Nile River

Blue Nile River

Ancient Egypt

0   250   500 km

The Bountiful Nile

The earliest Egyptians found that they could grow wheat, barley, and corn easily along the Nile. Over time they built efficient systems of dikes, irrigation ditches, and canals. These technologies trapped water for later use. They also prevented floodwaters from washing away the early settlements.

The Egyptians greatly respected the Nile—it was the heart of their culture. Besides providing food and sustenance, the river provided a convenient "highway" for boats. Here grew the vast stands of reeds that the Egyptians used to make **papyrus** [puh-PY-rus], a paper-like sheet for writing. The river also offered early Egyptians a place for entertainment and relaxation. Here people fished, rowed, swam, hunted for water birds, and played games.

According to Egyptian myth, Ra, the sun god, created the Nile. Egyptians believed that life began on a mound in the river.

Summer floods covered the valley floor.

The farmers harvested their grain.

The people tilled their fields and planted their crops in the moist soil.

Akhet Flood Time	June, July, August, September
Shemu Harvest Time	May, April, March
Peret Sowing Time	October, November, December, January, February

Egyptian life hummed to the rhythm of the Nile. The river's flooding cycle was so predictable that the Egyptians developed a calendar based on it. Why might ancient Egyptians name the times of the year after the three stages of the farming/flooding cycle?

Egypt: Gift of the Nile | 89

Rich Land, Rich Culture

The land along the Nile provided what was needed for a rich **culture** to flourish. A culture is the way of life shared by a group of people. It includes everything the people have, think, and do as members of an organized group, including how they make a living, their arts and music, and their institutions, traditions, and ceremonies. All groups have a culture, whether they live in a rural village or in downtown Vancouver. Here are some of the ways we can look at the culture of ancient Egypt.

Using this culture web as a guide, decide in which category each of these actions belongs: developing class rules, carving a totem pole, and making cookies.

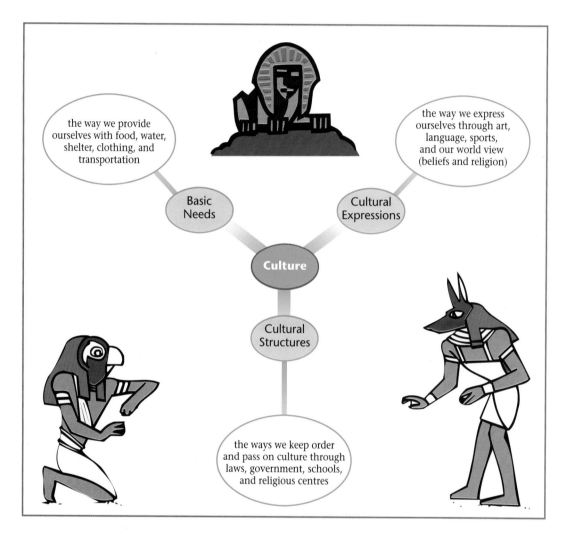

the way we provide ourselves with food, water, shelter, clothing, and transportation

the way we express ourselves through art, language, sports, and our world view (beliefs and religion)

Basic Needs

Cultural Expressions

Culture

Cultural Structures

the ways we keep order and pass on culture through laws, government, schools, and religious centres

Think For Yourself

Pick one of the following to discuss in a group:

"Egypt was 'the gift of the Nile'."

"The geography of Egypt influenced its culture."

With your group, decide if you agree or disagree with your chosen statement. Be prepared to support your group's opinion with evidence.

Meeting Basic Needs

Rich or poor, all people have ways to meet their basic needs. We sometimes call this "making a living." Cultures survive only when everyone can meet their basic needs.

Free Hands

In Egypt, the success of farming brought great developments. While many Egyptians continued to work in the field, some became skilled craftspeople making fine linen, wall hangings, wall paintings, pottery, fabric, tools of stone and metal, and luxury goods. New **engineering** and building techniques transformed the settlements into great cities. The valuable goods the cities produced allowed trade. This further increased Egypt's wealth and brought new goods—and new comforts—to the people.

Keeping Track of Wealth

As the wealth of Egypt grew and the economy became more complex, people needed a way to keep track of their wealth.

They developed a system of writing called **hieroglyphics** [hy-roe-GLIF-iks]. Hieroglyphs are little pictures. Some pictures stand for both an object and a sound. For example, a picture of an ox meant "ox." It also stood for the sound of the word.

Writing opened doors for the Egyptians. Besides recording business dealings, people began to write poetry, magic spells, and stories. They also recorded their knowledge, which later civilizations read about and learned from.

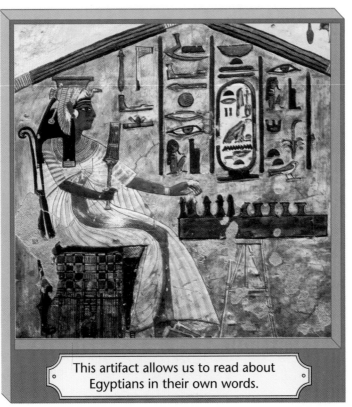

This artifact allows us to read about Egyptians in their own words.

Engineering means putting science to practical use.

Egyptians wrote on papyrus, but much of the hieroglyphic writing that survived was painted or carved on the stone walls of tombs. These hieroglyphics are painted on a picture of Nefertari playing chess. Compare these hieroglyphics with the Mesopotamian cuneiform letters on page 82.

To prepare and store food, people used clay jars, bowls, pots, pans, ladles, sieves, and whisks. What we know about Egyptian kitchen utensils comes from the items found in tombs.

The Family

The family unit is the basic building block of a culture. In ancient Egypt, the family provided security, food, and shelter. Through the family, children learned how to behave, the rules of society, and the beliefs, customs, and traditions of their culture.

At Home with Ordinary People

Slaves lived in the homes of their owners, but other ordinary people lived with their families in simple homes. Wood was rare in Egypt, so people built their homes from bricks of sun-dried mud, called **adobe** [uh-DOBE-ee]. Ordinary people lived in townhouses usually two or three storeys high. A business usually occupied the ground floor, and the family occupied the second and third floors. During summer, many people slept on the roof to keep cool.

The Egyptians had plenty of food, so even ordinary people enjoyed a healthy diet. They ate bread, beans, onions, leeks, and other vegetables, as well as fruit and fish from the Nile. Meat was expensive because land was needed for growing crops. Nonetheless, ordinary people occasionally ate pork. Most people drank beer made from barley bread.

People cooked in clay ovens or outdoors over open fires. They used wood for fuel, even though it was scarce. To make bread, women ground wheat into flour. Men then pounded the flour to make a fine grain. They mixed the grain with water, yeast, and salt to make dough. They often added sesame seeds, honey, fruit, butter, or herbs to the dough before baking it in clay ovens.

In ordinary families, the mother raised and cared for the children. Sons learned their father's trade, while daughters learned the skills needed to run a household. Neither boys nor girls of ordinary families learned to read and write.

At Home with the Rich

The homes of the nobles were large, with a reception hall, private rooms for the man of the house, and private rooms for the women and children. Despite the size of these homes, they were still made with adobe. (Only temples and tombs were made of stone.) The windows and doors were covered with mats to keep out the flies, dust, and heat. People decorated the inside walls with colourful wall hangings and covered the floors with tile.

Wealthy people had slaves and servants who cooked, cleaned, shopped, and helped take care of the children. Boys went to school in the temple or took their lessons from **tutors**, private teachers. They had to learn hundreds of hieroglyphs as well as complicated arithmetic.

Wealthy people ate bread, vegetables, and fruit, as did ordinary people. Unlike ordinary people, however, the rich could afford roast beef and wine. The wealthy ate from dishes made of bronze, silver, and gold. Like all Egyptians, they ate with their fingers.

Try This

1. Make a list of different ways that the ancient Egyptians made a living to help them meet their basic needs. Compare your list with the ways that people meet their needs in your community.

2. Join with other classmates to form one of three groups. One group will be an ordinary ancient Egyptian family. Another will be a rich ancient Egyptian family. The third group will be a modern Canadian family. With your group, dramatize or illustrate the preparation and sharing of an evening meal.

Both women and men could earn money and own property. Either could ask for a divorce or fight a divorce. A divorced woman could keep her children and property and marry again.

Cultural Expressions

The greatness of ancient Egypt is found in the expression of its culture. People show their culture through their art and language as well as through their beliefs, religion, and traditions. The Egyptians left us a rich record of their unique culture.

The people of ancient Egypt lived a life we recognize—it's much like our own. Egyptians enjoyed games, music and entertainment, jewellery, art and music, and comfortable homes. In other words, they had a highly developed culture.

Fashion in Ancient Egypt

One very personal form of cultural expression is the way we adorn ourselves. We all express ourselves through the clothing, jewellery, and make-up we wear, and the way we wear our hair. Ancient Egyptians did just the same.

This painting from the wall of a tomb shows Nefertari, an Egyptian queen, dressed in her everyday clothing. Spot three ways that she adorns herself.

Make-up

Ancient Egyptians felt it was important to boost their personal beauty. Men, women, and children of all ages and classes wore make-up. Every morning they would peer into their mirrors of highly polished silver or copper. They outlined their eyes and darkened their eyelashes using **kohl** [KOLE], a black powder mixed with water. They applied a red clay called **ochre** [OKE-ur] to their lips and cheeks. Using **henna** [HEN-uh], a plant dye, they coloured their fingernails yellow or orange.

Hairstyles

People wore their hair in styles that were very similar to our own. Ordinary people wore their hair short. Girls usually wore pigtails while boys had shaved heads, except for one braided lock worn to one side. Some men and women dyed their hair using henna. Others—both men and women—wore wigs made of sheep's wool or human hair, both for the effect and to protect themselves from the heat. They stored their wigs in special boxes on a stand inside their homes.

Jewellery

Egyptians loved wearing jewellery. They thought that rings and **amulets** [AM-yoo-lets] (good-luck charms) could keep away evil spirits and prevent injury. Both men and women wore pierced earrings, armlets, bracelets, and anklets. Wealthy people wore jewelled or beaded collars, necklaces, and pendants of precious stones and metals. Ordinary people made do with jewellery created from less valuable materials.

Clothing

People dressed for comfort in Egypt's hot, dry climate. Most clothing was made of white linen, a cloth made from the fibres of the flax plant. For women, the linen **shift** (a simple, loose-fitting dress) was standard for nearly a thousand years. Wealthy women sometimes wore a transparent covering on top. Men wore **loincloths**, or wrap-around skirts. Those who could not afford expensive, finely woven linen wore coarsely woven linen. Most people went barefoot, but wore sandals on special occasions.

Besides helping Egyptians look beautiful, kohl helped fight eye infections and reduced the glare of the brilliant Egyptian sun.

Try This

Meet in a small group to discuss the following: Compare the ways that Egyptians adorned themselves with the way you and your friends do. Consider hairstyle, make-up, jewellery, clothing, and footwear. Make a Venn diagram like the one shown here to help organize your thinking.

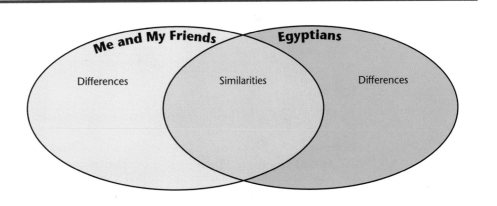

Me and My Friends — Differences

Similarities

Egyptians — Differences

Religion in Ancient Egypt

Another form of cultural expression is a society's beliefs and religion. These are expressions of the people's **world view**.

People of ancient Egypt worshipped hundreds of gods and goddesses, or **deities** [DEE-ih-teez]. Some were common to all of Egypt. Others were worshipped only in one city. Some of the gods depicted in Egyptian legends had animal heads and human bodies, such as Horus, the falcon-headed god. All were powerful.

Egyptians believed that almost everything that happened in their daily lives resulted from the actions of gods or goddesses. They gave credit to them for the regular flooding of the Nile, the enormous size and harshness of the surrounding desert, and the daily rising and setting of the sun. People believed that any misfortunes or fortunes encountered in their lives came about because a deity had willed it. People feared their deities and worshipped regularly to keep them happy. For example, to ensure the yearly life-giving flood of the Nile, people made offerings to the deities of the sun, moon, earth, and water.

Life After Death

All ancient Egyptians believed in the **afterlife**—a happy continuation of life on earth with all it pleasures. Egyptians spent their lives preparing for the afterlife. **Pharaohs** [FAIR-oze],

Horus
Sky God

Seth
Brother and Enemy of Horus

Thoth
God of Writing, Counting, and Wisdom

Khnum
Creator God

Hathor
Goddess of Women

Sobek
God of the Faiyum Region

Egyptian kings, built fine tombs and collected beautiful treasures to store with their mummified bodies. Others prepared for their afterlives in more affordable ways. Many tombs were filled with models, drawings, sculptures, and paintings representing real things. To protect the deceased in the afterlife, the Egyptians carved his or her name in the tomb.

To get into the afterlife, Egyptians believed that the dead person would first be judged by Osiris, god of the underworld. In a ritual known as the weighing of the heart, the deceased sums up his or her life. For example, the person might say such things as "I have not told lies. I have not stolen food." Osiris would decide if the person had led a worthy life, and could therefore enter the afterlife. A papyrus *Book of the Dead* contains the spells and rituals that priests used to ensure that people passed the test.

To remain in the afterlife, Egyptians believed they needed a "home" for their spirit here on earth—they needed an intact human body. To keep the corpses of the dead from rotting, Egyptians learned how to **embalm** [em-BOM] them. Embalming is a technique for preserving the human corpse. Egyptians specialized in **mummification** [muh-mih-fih-KAY-shun], one form of embalming. At first it was available only to pharaohs. Eventually everyone could enjoy the privilege.

Ra
The Sun God

Amun
Sun God who became linked to Ra

Anubis
God of Mummification

Osiris
The God of Vegetation and the Ruler of the Underworld

Isis
Wife of Osiris and Mistress of Magic

A Closer Look

How to Make a Mummy

The entire process of mummification took 70 days to complete. Several embalmers worked together on the task. The chief embalmer wore a jackal mask to represent Anubis, the god of mummification. The embalming process involved the following basic steps.

- All of the internal organs, except the heart, were removed. The heart was left in the body because Egyptians believed it was the organ that contained all intelligence and emotion. The removed organs were mummified and put in jars that were placed in the tomb at the time of burial. The brain was thought to be useless. They removed it by scooping it out with a wire through the nose. Then the mouth was cleaned out and filled with sweet, oil-scented linen.

- The body was packed and covered with **natron**, a salty drying agent, and was left to dry out. After 40 to 50 days, all the body's liquids would have been absorbed. Only the hair, skin, and bones would be left.

- The body cavity was then stuffed with resin, sawdust, or linen and shaped to restore the form and features of the dead person. Then the embalmers sewed up the body. They put onions or painted white stones into the eye sockets, and put beeswax in the nostrils. Then they filled up the spaces where the organs once were with spices and herbs.

- Finally, the body was tightly wrapped in many layers of linen. After the wrapping was complete, the body was put into a burial sheet called a **shroud** [SHROWD] and placed in a stone coffin called a **sarcophagus** [sar-KOF-uh-gus].

The final stage of the mummification process. The embalmers put jewellery and amulets between the layers of linen. They place a scarab-beetle amulet over the heart. At each stage of wrapping, a priest chants spells and prayers.

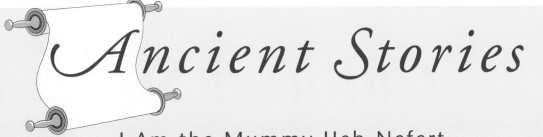

Ancient Stories

I Am the Mummy Heb-Nefert

Historical fiction and poetry tell about fictional people in a real time and place from the past. The best historical fiction and historical poetry get the facts right. With the right facts, readers can understand what life was like at the time and how people lived and died. This poem is about a fictional Egyptian woman. Heb-Nefert [HEB NEF-urt] dies and describes her own embalming—she becomes a mummy. As you read, notice the factual information the poet used to tell Heb-Nefert's story.

I am the mummy Heb-Nefert,…
Once I was the daughter of a nomarch,
favoured, beautiful.
But all things change.…
I rose above myself
and watched.
I watched as they
anointed me with oils and spices,
took away the parts of me
that were inside,
and filled me up
with natron, cinnamon, and herbs.
My eyes were closed and plugged.
Beeswax filled my nose.
They capped my nails with gold
studded with precious stones,
bejewelled me head to toe,
and bound me in linen,
layer on layer.
I was to be
for all eternity
well kept for him.
They made me a mask
painted to look like me,
bound up my cat and masked her too
my faithful cat, Nebut [nay-BOOT].
Placed me in my sarcophagus
pictured round with likenesses
of gods who would receive me.

Excerpts from Eve Bunting, *I Am the Mummy Heb-Nefert*,
(Toronto: Harcourt Inc., 1997)

Try This

Compare the information about embalming in the Closer Look feature on page 98 and in the poem on this page. What parts of the poem are facts and what parts are details the poet imagined about Heb-Nefert?

Cultural Structures

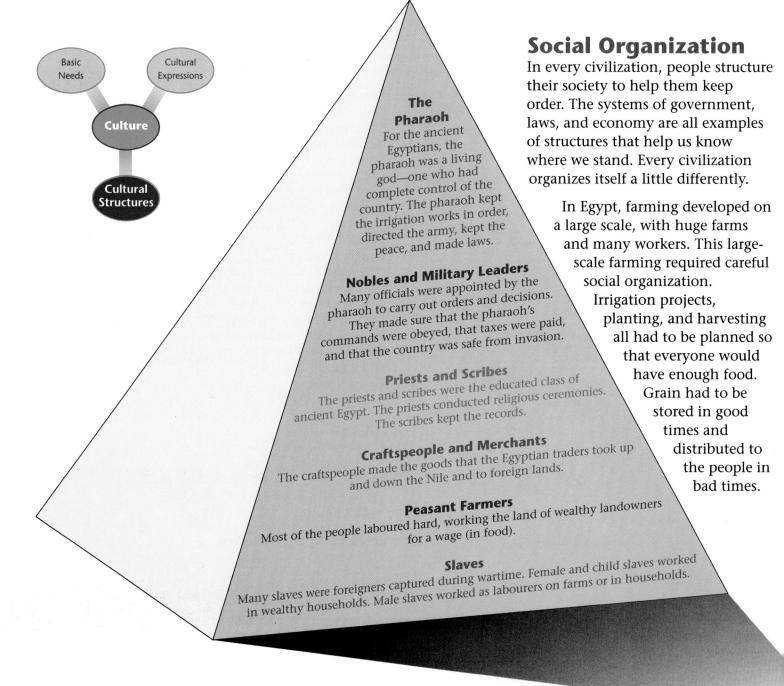

Basic Needs · **Cultural Expressions** · **Culture** · **Cultural Structures**

The Pharaoh
For the ancient Egyptians, the pharaoh was a living god—one who had complete control of the country. The pharaoh kept the irrigation works in order, directed the army, kept the peace, and made laws.

Nobles and Military Leaders
Many officials were appointed by the pharaoh to carry out orders and decisions. They made sure that the pharaoh's commands were obeyed, that taxes were paid, and that the country was safe from invasion.

Priests and Scribes
The priests and scribes were the educated class of ancient Egypt. The priests conducted religious ceremonies. The scribes kept the records.

Craftspeople and Merchants
The craftspeople made the goods that the Egyptian traders took up and down the Nile and to foreign lands.

Peasant Farmers
Most of the people laboured hard, working the land of wealthy landowners for a wage (in food).

Slaves
Many slaves were foreigners captured during wartime. Female and child slaves worked in wealthy households. Male slaves worked as labourers on farms or in households.

Social Organization
In every civilization, people structure their society to help them keep order. The systems of government, laws, and economy are all examples of structures that help us know where we stand. Every civilization organizes itself a little differently.

In Egypt, farming developed on a large scale, with huge farms and many workers. This large-scale farming required careful social organization. Irrigation projects, planting, and harvesting all had to be planned so that everyone would have enough food. Grain had to be stored in good times and distributed to the people in bad times.

With a large population living along the narrow strip of fertile land, disputes sometimes broke out. Laws helped settle these disputes. So did a social order that said who had power over whom. Organization was very important in ensuring that society would be stable and life would be good for everyone.

Central Power

In Egypt, the word of the pharaoh was law. The very early pharaohs were believed to be Horus, the Sky God, in human shape, and a descendant of the supreme sun god, Ra. All pharaohs were considered to be gods. Writing on the walls of the Pyramid of Unas said as much:

*Behold, the king is at the head of the gods.... The gods do **obeisance** [oh-BAY-sunts] when meeting the king just as the gods do obeisance when meeting the rising of Ra when he ascends from the horizon.*

Because the pharaoh was considered to be a god on earth, everyone obeyed the pharaoh's commands. These all-powerful rulers controlled all the land, all the trade, and all the people. Through their government officials,

the pharaohs supervised irrigation and controlled where people lived. Through their generals, the pharaohs controlled the armies. Through their **nomarchs** [NOME-arks] (tax collectors), they took the largest share of the crops grown along the Nile.

On the one hand, the power of the pharaohs made great achievements possible. This benefited many of the people. If the pharaoh wanted grain stored for hard times, it was collected. If the pharaoh wanted an army to attack an invader, it was done. On the other hand, if a pharaoh wanted someone dead, he or she was killed on the spot.

The word **pharaoh** comes from the Egyptian word meaning "great house." The ancient Egyptians showed respect for the king by referring to the palace instead of using his or her name.

To "do obeisance" is to bow or submit.

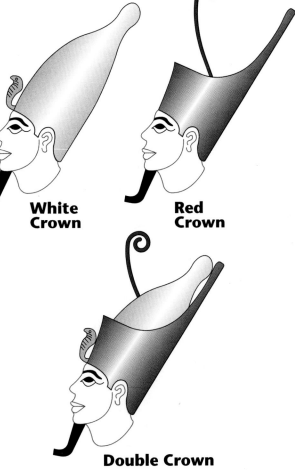

White Crown

Red Crown

Double Crown

Rulers of Upper Egypt (southern Egypt) wore a white crown and those of Lower Egypt (northern Egypt) wore a red crown. After the two kingdoms were united, the pharaohs wore a double crown to show that they ruled both regions.

The Great Pyramid of Giza [GEE-zuh] was built to hold the tomb of the Pharaoh Khufu [KHOFE-oo]. It is still one of the largest structures ever built by humans. Each limestone building block weighed between 2 and 15 tonnes. Over two million of these were cut, moved, and set in place by workers—without any help from computer design programs, machinery, electricity, fossil fuels, or even metal tools.

Public works are huge building projects that benefit the general public, such as bridges, dams, and museums. Monuments are structures built to help us remember.

The great pyramids of Egypt housed the tombs of the pharaohs. The tomb itself was very tiny. Why do you think the pharaohs wanted such massive buildings as their burial places?

The pharaohs of Egypt used their great wealth to build great temples, **public works**, and **monuments** [MON-yoo-ments] to themselves. The result was some of the most spectacular monuments ever built. Thousands and thousands of construction workers, stone cutters, sculptors, painters, and labourers did the work.

Having a strong central power over centuries brought stability to the land and allowed traditions to develop. People gave attention to the development of music, mythology, law, writing, and other things that improved their quality of life.

King's chamber

Air channel

Grand gallery

Abandoned chambers

Narrow escape tunnel

A Closer Look

Akhenaten

Akhenaten, sometimes known as the Rebel Pharaoh, ruled for 17 years (1352 BCE–1336 BCE). During his rule, Egypt was more powerful than it had ever been. When he gained power, his name was Amenhotep IV. About four years into his reign, he changed his name to Akhenaten. At the same time he tried to change ancient Egypt, a society that prided itself on the ideals of tradition and stability.

Akhenaten influenced the style of art and architecture. He encouraged artists to make their art less stylized and more realistic. For a time, this freed artists and craftspeople from traditional forms. They could explore their creativity in any way they chose.

Akhenaten replaced the many gods and goddesses of ancient Egypt with one god, Aten. Aten showed himself as the sun disk. Akhenaten said he was the only person who could contact the new god.

This made priests unnecessary, and Akhenaten took all their property.

After Akhenaten's death, his religion was abandoned. The new pharaoh turned back to the traditional gods and goddesses, and the priests came back to power. The high-priest had Akhenaten's name erased from monuments.

Akhenaten did leave an invaluable legacy. When archaeologists excavated the abandoned palace, they found 350 letters. These letters tell us much about political life in Egypt at this time.

The statue of Tutmose III, at left, was created in the traditional Egyptian style. The relief of Akhenaten, below, shows the realistic style Akhenaten encouraged.

This three-storied funeral temple, called Deir el-Bahri [DAYR el-BAY-hair-ee], is dedicated to Amon [AH-moon] and Hathor [hah-THOOR]. It was one of the great building projects of Hatshepsut [hah-chep-SOOT], the first woman to be pharaoh. Four of the pharaohs of ancient Egypt were women.

The Canadian Charter of Rights and Freedoms guarantees Canadians freedom of religion, thought, belief, opinion, and expression. Having such freedoms gives us control to make decisions about our lives. Having such freedoms also increases our responsibilities.

Think For Yourself

1. "Egypt became a great civilization because the pharaohs were great and powerful leaders." Do you agree or disagree with this statement? Give at least two reasons to support your opinion.

2. In Egypt, the pharaoh made laws to control people. Explain the advantages and disadvantages, to the state and to individuals, of having laws that control all aspects of a person's life.

Legacy of Egypt

Culture and civilization are closely related. It is a people's culture, or way of life, that allows a civilization to develop. In turn, a strong civilization will provide **continuity** [kon-tih-NYOO-ih-tee], the long-term stability and security that allows a culture to flourish. Only with continuity can people pass on their achievements—their **legacy** [LEG-uh-see]—to the next generation. The ancient Egyptian culture was exceptional partly because the Egyptians had one of the longest-lasting civilizations in history.

What is the meaning of the word *civilization*? **Civilization** can be defined in many ways. At its simplest, *civilization* describes a large, organized society that has lasted a long time. Organization allows a very large number of people to live together peacefully. Canada's systems of schooling and garbage collection are both examples of organization. These systems benefit everyone in society.

Most early civilizations arose in cities. The English words *city* and *civilization* both come from the Latin word *civis*, which means "home." For early people, the city was the home of those who were civilized. City dwellers didn't have to work in the fields. Instead, they learned new skills through their work and also at school. Over time, cities became very powerful. Law, religion, written language, and the arts all developed and flourished in the cities.

Historians have identified the features common to all the highly organized societies we call civilizations. When we consider these features together, we can see how they allow certain societies to achieve great things.

A legacy is something that one generation leaves for those who follow. World civilization is the product of earlier civilizations and their legacies to us.

A civilization can contain one culture or several, as in Canada's multicultural society.

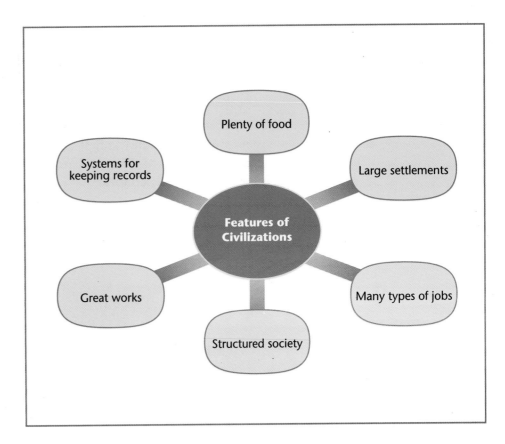

For black ink, the Egyptians ground charcoal with water. For red ink, they used ochre, a type of red earth. Their pens were cut from reeds, with the end sharpened to a point, forming a **nib**.

Features of Civilization

- *Plenty of food:* Civilizations must have plenty of food. Extra food is stored for lean times or is traded for goods.

- *Large settlements:* Large populations living together in towns and cities can protect themselves from enemies. To live together peacefully, the people find ways to work out their differences.

- *Many types of jobs:* When only part of the population needs to farm the land, new occupations become possible. Craftspeople, teachers, soldiers, traders, and artists are some of the workers needed for a civilization to thrive.

- *Structured society:* When large numbers of people live together they need social structures that clarify who has power. In the ancient world, those with military might usually controlled the wealth and the people.

- *Great works:* The great buildings, art, monuments, and public works of a civilization are symbols of its greatness. They become possible when labour is available, and when government can organize projects on a grand scale.

- *Systems for keeping records:* As wealth grows, people need ways to keep records of what they own, and what they buy and sell. The government needs a way to record each person's contributions—what they pay through taxes. Early record-keeping systems often led to other types of written records, such as laws, historical records, and literature.

Try This

Use the web on the previous page to develop a "Features of Egyptian Civilization" chart. In the first column, list each feature of civilization. Head the second column with "Egypt." You can fill up the chart by reviewing the information in this chapter.

Features of Civilization	Egypt

Investigate

Working in a group, choose one of the features from the Features of Civilizations web on page 105. Research an example of that feature from ancient Egypt. Before beginning your research, follow these steps.

- Look through this chapter and at other resources about Egypt to get ideas for a topic.

- Read "How to Refine a Research Topic" on the next page.

- Look back at "How to Research" on pages 3–4 in Chapter 1.

- Choose the best format to get your ideas across. It might be a poster, computer presentation, or pamphlet.

Think For Yourself

We have said that Egypt had a great culture. What made it great? What was its greatest legacy? This could be something concrete or something abstract. Prepare a description, replica, or illustration of your choice. Be prepared to present it to the class, giving a brief history of your choice, describing how it influenced the people of Egypt, and stating your reasons for choosing it as the greatest achievement of ancient Egypt.

 Credit Sources

Clearly identifying sources helps you get organized. By keeping track of where you found your information, you can create a **bibliography** [bib-lee-AH-gruf-ee]—a list of the sources you used. For each source you use, record the following information.

- The full name of the author. If there is more than one author, record all the names.
- The full title.
- The place of publication and the name of the publisher.
- The date of publication. You'll find this on the copyright page with a copyright symbol (©) beside it.
- The page numbers where you found your information.

When you put it all together, it should look like this:

Toutant, Arnold, and Susan Doyle. *Ancient Worlds*. Toronto: Oxford University Press, 2000, p. 107.

HOW TO... Refine a Research Topic

A topic has to be manageable. In other words, you have to be able to research it well in the time you have. If your topic is too big, you could still be doing the research when you graduate from high school! Here are some tips for narrowing your topic.

1. Start with a broad, general topic.

2. Now brainstorm some subtopics. For example, if your topic is "The Monumental Works of Egypt," your list of subtopics might include "pyramids," "irrigation," and "temples."

3. Select one of the subtopics, and use it to generate even more specific topics. For example, let's use "pyramids" as your subtopic. A list of specific topics might include
   - Why the pyramids were built
   - How the Great Pyramid was built
   - Good and bad aspects of building pyramids

4. Before settling on your specific topic, discuss it with others who can help you decide if it's manageable. Before starting your research, look over general references to help you refine your topic further.

Looking Back

In this chapter, you have learned about basic needs, cultural expressions, and cultural structures as they existed in ancient Egypt. You have also seen that ancient Egypt had the features that all civilizations share. What do you find most impressive about ancient Egyptian civilization?

Chapter 6

India: Land of Diversity

What do you think life will be like in Canada in 100 years? How about in 5000? Will Canada be a mighty empire? Will Canada even exist as a nation? Five thousand years ago, the people of ancient India might have wondered about their future too. Little did they know that civilization in India would flourish for a time, crash, and eventually flourish again.

Every civilization, including Canada's and India's, has a unique story. All of these stories finish up with one of three possible endings: the civilization survives, it gets absorbed by another civilization, or it disappears. Why do some civilizations last while others do not?

In this chapter, you can learn about the civilization of India, one of the world's most ancient cultures. Perhaps more than any other, India's civilization has gone through many changes, rising and falling and rising again. As you read about India, think about what India's story tells you about how civilizations survive.

An Inviting Land

India is a subcontinent—a large, geographically separate section of a continent. Two of its three sides are bordered by water, making it a **peninsula** [pen-IN-syoo-luh]. Mountains border its third side, to the north.

People have always moved in search of better places to live. In ancient times they travelled in search of warm weather, fertile soil, and plentiful food. The land of ancient India had all of these in abundance. So, despite a vast mountainous barrier, India attracted people like a magnet.

India's location in South Asia meant that people came from cultures to the east, west, and north. For almost 7000 years, India has been welcoming people of different races, beliefs, and languages, creating a culture of incredible variety. The Indian **subcontinent** was so large that it could easily take in many people. It was one of the first lands to support large populations.

The two highest mountain ranges in the world—the Himalayas and the Hindu Kush—stretch along India's northern border. Here you can see Mount Kanchenjunga from the Indian side of the mountain range. Mountains like these formed a towering barrier, dividing India from the rest of the continent.

A Better Home

Humans have been making a home in India for at least 400 000 years. Archaeologists know little about the early life of the very first inhabitants—the **Aboriginal** [ab-uh-RIJ-uh-nal] people of India. Small pockets of these ancient people, called Adivasis [ad-ee-VAH-seez], have survived in India, especially in the remote hill country.

The earliest people to settle in India were nomadic herding people. They brought their animals down from their mountain homes during the winter months to escape the harsh winds and snow. As they moved south, the people discovered a rich **alluvial** [uh-LOO-vee-ul] plain—a land made fertile by the silt brought down by three rivers: the Indus, the Brahmaputra, and the Ganges. Besides having rich soil, renewed every year by river flooding, the plain enjoys generous seasonal rains.

Over time, these nomadic visitors stayed on through the summer months. They began to use the river water to irrigate farms. They built up prosperous and long-lasting settlements. The population grew steadily as waves of migrating people entered India from the neighbouring lands. Most settlers entered through mountain passes. Later, seafaring peoples travelled across the Arabian Sea and settled on both the west and east coasts. Since its very beginning, India has always supported a large population made up of many different peoples.

Even today, India's fertile northern plain is one of the richest agricultural areas in the world. Since ancient times, it has provided food for millions of people.

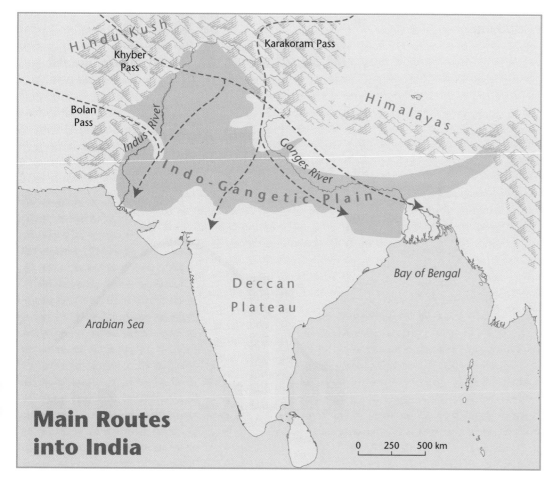

Main Routes into India

Hindu Kush
Khyber Pass
Karakoram Pass
Bolan Pass
Indus River
Himalayas
Ganges River
Indo-Gangetic Plain
Deccan Plateau
Bay of Bengal
Arabian Sea

0   250   500 km

After crossing the mountains, settlers came to the fertile northern plain of India—called the Indo-Gangetic [in-doe-gan-JET-ik] Plain. What might they have thought when they saw it for the first time?

Try This

1. Examine the two climagraphs shown here. One shows the climate information of Kabul, Afghanistan. Kabul lies in the Hindu Kush Mountains to the northwest of India. The other climagraph shows the climate information of New Delhi, India's capital city. New Delhi lies on the Indo-Gangetic Plain.
Compare the climagraph for New Delhi with the climagraph for Kabul. Write a brief description of the seasons in the two cities.

2. Find both New Delhi and Kabul on a map of Southeast Asia. Use their location to help you explain why each area has the climate it has.

3. Describe how the climate in each area would affect people's ability to meet their needs for food, shelter, and clothing.

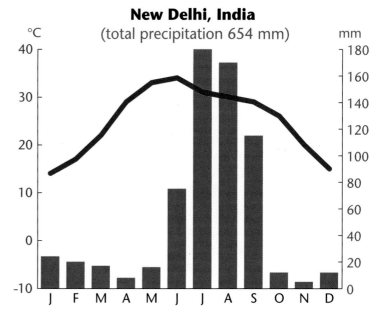

New Delhi, India
(total precipitation 654 mm)

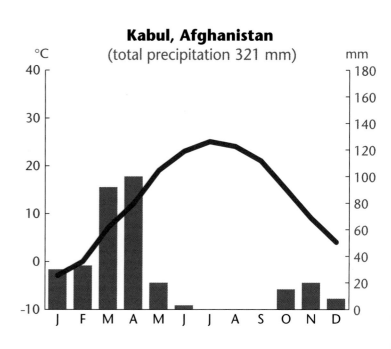

Kabul, Afghanistan
(total precipitation 321 mm)

The Indus Valley Civilization

The stories of many ancient civilizations end in mystery. All around the world, archaeologists have found the remains of civilizations that vanished, leaving only a few clues. Often all that's left is rubble.

The Indus Valley civilization—India's first civilization—is a mystery like that. It began about 5000 years ago, when the early people of India began to settle in towns and cities along the Indus River valley. By 2500 BCE a great civilization had grown up. It stretched along the Indus River valley, linking many large towns and cities. It lasted for 1000 years, and then disappeared.

Planned Cities

All the evidence points to a thriving culture that had much in common with the early civilizations of Mesopotamia and Egypt. But the Indus Valley cities were different in a remarkable way. They seem to have been designed for the comfort of the people who lived in them rather than for the glory of kings.

The people who built the Indus Valley cities must have included engineers and town planners. Every town was laid out in straight lines.

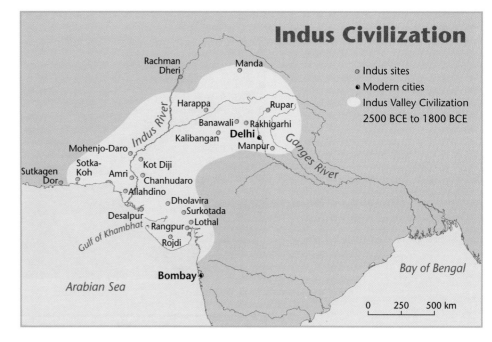

Indus Civilization

- Indus sites
- Modern cities
- Indus Valley Civilization 2500 BCE to 1800 BCE

Rachman Dheri, Manda, Harappa, Rupar, Banawali, Rakhigarhi, Kalibangan, Delhi, Mohenjo-Daro, Manpur, Sotka-Koh, Kot Diji, Sutkagen Dor, Amri, Chanhudaro, Allahdino, Dholavira, Surkotada, Desalpur, Lothal, Rangpur, Rojdi, Bombay

Indus River, Ganges River, Arabian Sea, Gulf of Khambhat, Bay of Bengal

0   250   500 km

The Indus Valley people were the first to design their towns before building them.

Buildings were made of a standard-sized brick. This means the people must have had some system of measurement. The houses were all one or two storeys high, with flat roofs. All houses were just about identical. Each home had its own private drinking well and its own private bathroom. Clay pipes led from the bathrooms to sewers located under the streets. Sanitation systems like these must have kept diseases under control in the hot climate of northern India.

Over 1400 sites have been discovered in what are now Pakistan, India, and Afghanistan. Using the scale on the map, figure out the approximate area of the Indus Valley civilization. How does it compare in size to British Columbia (947 800 km^2)?

The ancient script of the Indus Valley people has never been decoded.

Archaeologists have found no temples or palaces like those found in Mesopotamia and Egypt. Most public buildings in the city seem to have been built to improve life for the people. These include giant public baths like the one shown here.

The ruins of the Indus Valley civilization were only discovered in the past century.

Think For Yourself

We don't usually think about sewage systems when we think about the idea of progress. But sewage systems are one of the most important ways of improving daily life for people.

1. With a partner, brainstorm a list of skills and social structures that a people would need before they could develop sewage systems. To help organize your ideas, create a chart with the following headings: Skills, Technology, Social Organization, and Economy.

2. Review the features of civilization on page 106 in Chapter 5. Decide if you agree or disagree with this statement: "Sewage systems are a mark of civilization." State your position and explain your reasons.

City Life

The people of the Indus Valley must have been very good farmers. They grew barley, peas, melons, wheat, and dates. Each town had a large central storage building for grain. These granaries used an ingenious method of circulating air so the food would stay dry during the rainy season. Evidence shows that the people grew cotton and made it into cloth. They may have been the first people to do so.

The people kept many tame animals. They had herds of cattle, sheep, pigs, and water buffalo, and even cats and dogs. In one excavated site, the footprints of a cat were found, followed right behind by those of a dog.

This artifact shows the type of dress and body ornaments worn in the Indus Valley.

The people of the Indus Valley wore colourful cotton clothing. Notice the design on the clothing of the man pictured here. Women wore jewellery of gold and precious stones, and lipstick.

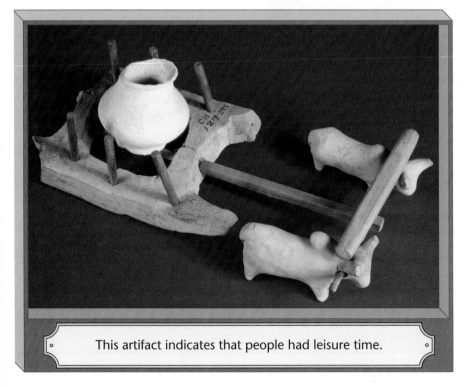

This artifact indicates that people had leisure time.

Among the treasures found in Mohenjo-Daro [muh-HENJ-oe DAR-oe] was the statue of a woman wearing a bracelet. Bracelets with similar designs are worn today in India.

The people of the Indus Valley made many toys like this small cart for their children. Excavators have found whistles shaped like birds and toy monkeys. What skills are required to make these toys?

India: Land of Diversity | **115**

The god in a seated, cross-legged position appears in artwork in the Indus Valley civilization. This may be an early form of Shiva [SHEE-vuh], who later became one of the important gods of Hinduism. That makes Shiva the longest-worshipped god in history.

Seals like these are a real mystery. They were carved from soapstone, and then pressed into soft clay. People used them to mark the goods they traded. Archaeologists have found similar seals in Mesopotamia, which suggests there was trade between these civilizations.

These artifacts show us how the Indus Valley script looked.

We know that Indus Valley towns were designed on a grid of straight lines. This tells us that some people may have made a living as engineers or town planners.

Try This

1. Using pages 113–16, make a list of facts archaeologists have learned about the Indus Valley civilization. Make a two-column chart listing your facts in the left column. Think about how each fact suggests a possible way of making a living. List these in the right column. Your chart can begin like the one shown here.

Facts About the Indus Valley Civilization	Possible Ways of Making a Living
• bricks were a standard size	• laying bricks
• people wore colourful cotton clothing	• farming cotton, weaving cloth, dying cloth

2. Make a chart comparing how the people of Mesopotamia, Egypt, and the Indus Valley civilization met common needs. Be sure to compare how the people got food, got water, clothed themselves, and built their shelters.

A Gradual Ending

The Indus Valley civilization ended about 1500 BCE. Its end wasn't a sudden event. Instead, the highly organized way of life gradually fell apart over several centuries. By the last years of the civilization, the pottery and sculpture had a much simpler style. The buildings were no longer carefully planned and built. Everything, it seems, began to decline.

Here are some of the changes scientists think may have contributed to the decline of the Indus Valley civilization.

- Climate change may have caused the rains to move to the east, away from the Indus Valley.

- Farmers may have stripped the soil of its nutrients over centuries of farming.

- Irrigation may have poisoned the soil with salt, as it did in Mesopotamia.

- Herds of sheep and goats may have stripped the hillsides of plants, causing erosion.

- People needed wood for use as a building material and for firewood to bake bricks. Extensive logging may have destroyed the forests.

- Trading partners of the Indus Valley people were suffering economic declines. This may have caused the Indus Valley economy to crumble.

- Constant flooding of the Indus River may have made life in the cities impossible.

If an environmental change made life harder and harder for the people, they probably began to move in search of more productive land. Aggressive neighbours called Aryans may have taken advantage of the weakness—it was a good opportunity to invade a highly desirable land.

Try This

With a partner, make a graphic organizer to analyze the reasons for the decline of the Indus Valley civilization, as listed above. In your organizer, list each of the possible causes. Beside each cause, explain what effect it might have had. You can set up each cause and effect in boxes as shown here.

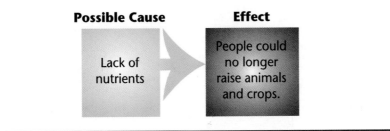

Possible Cause → **Effect**

Lack of nutrients → People could no longer raise animals and crops.

Ancient Mysteries

Mound of the Dead

The ancient city of Mohenjo-Daro was one of the first Indus Valley sites to be discovered, in what is now Pakistan. The discovery of this ancient city puzzled archaeologists. They had no knowledge of a civilization in ancient India.

Then the archaeologists began finding hundreds of other sites from the same time period. They "solved" the mystery of Mohenjo-Daro when they realized they were looking at evidence of a civilization they didn't know existed—the Indus Valley civilization. More sites appear every year. With each new discovery, our knowledge of what life was like in the Indus Valley becomes more complete.

Mohenjo-Daro was different from the other sites of the Indus Valley, however. Its name, Mohenjo-Daro, was not the city's original name. It means "mound of the dead." Archaeologists gave it this name after they found a pile of unburied skeletons. From a city that may have been home to as many as 80 000 people, nothing but rubble and a few skeletons remains. What happened to the population of the city? Why were bodies left untended? This may be a mystery archaeologists will never be able to solve.

What caused the end of Mohenjo-Daro? We may never know.

Strength in Differences

India's first civilization disappeared, but India's story didn't end there. A new civilization emerged that began a very long chapter in India's story—one that has lasted for 3500 years, right to the present day. Its story is one of survival.

The Hindu culture, as the main culture of India came to be known, had a unique approach to survival. Unlike many other ancient civilizations, India wasn't a land that could be ruled by one single way of life or set of beliefs. There were just too many new people constantly arriving—people of different ethnic backgrounds, with different languages, beliefs, and ways of living.

Instead, the new culture of India developed a way for all the different groups in India to preserve their own distinctive ways. At the same time each culture could contribute to the common good. This approach is often called "unity in **diversity**" [dih-VERS-ih-tee]. It has allowed the many cultures of India to keep their way of life alive in spite of the great changes that have happened over time.

A diverse country is one that has great variety.

Many new Canadians come from India. These two travel on a BC ferry. What makes ancient India and Canada similar to each other, and different from many other countries?

A Closer Look

India's Diversity

Since its earliest days, India has been one of the world's most multicultural countries. Here are a few of the people from modern India's many different cultures.

This Tamil woman works on a tea plantation in Sri Lanka. Her ancestors, the Dravidians, were the earliest people to travel south from the fertile northern plains.

These Sikhs live on the Indo-Gangetic plain. Most of the people who live on the plain today are descendants of the waves of immigrants who entered India from the northwest thousands of years ago.

India has about 50 million Adivasis, or Aboriginal people, whose ancestors were the subcontinent's earliest inhabitants. Many live in the few forests that are left. Laws protect their rights as minorities. Like the forests they live in, however, their traditional way of life is quickly disappearing.

These Kashmiri children live in northern India. Some of the people of the northern mountains are **Muslims** [MUZ-limz]. They follow the Islamic religion, like their neighbours in Pakistan and Afghanistan. Others are Hindu or Buddhist.

The desert people of Rajasthan [rah-juh-STAN] wear some of the most colourful clothing and elaborate jewellery in all of India. The people known in other parts of the world as Romanies, or Gypsies, have their origins in Rajasthan.

The people of Sikkim [SIK-im] are distant cousins of their Chinese neighbours. They live in a land of towering mountains.

As warriors, the Aryans had a great advantage over many other ancient peoples. They had light chariots drawn by fast, powerful horses. With this advantage they conquered lands from India to Europe.

The Ganges River became the centre of the Aryan culture, and was thought of as a holy river. Many of the people of India still believe that bathing in "Mother Ganges" purifies a person's soul.

India's Aryan Heritage

We don't know for sure what caused the peaceful civilization of the Indus Valley to disappear. But we do know that around the time that the Indus Valley civilization ended, waves of new settlers swept south into India from central Asia.

The settlers called themselves **Aryans** [AIR-ee-unz], which means "noble ones." They did not have the advanced knowledge or technology of the people of the Indus Valley cities. They were a nomadic, warrior people. After settling into villages, they tended large herds of animals, carrying on their traditional life as a farming people.

The Aryans gradually settled the land from the Indus Valley to the Ganges Valley. Over the next thousand years they developed a new culture based on a set of common beliefs.

Common Beliefs

How do people live together without fighting? Large organized religions help solve the problem. They help strangers live together without fighting. The beliefs of the Aryans became a great unifying force in India. They helped different peoples live together in peace.

The beliefs of the Aryans were similar to those of other ancient peoples. Priests sacrificed animals as offerings to the gods. The people worshipped nature and took part in elaborate ceremonies. Some of these ceremonies were very old, going back to the earliest days of the Aryan culture. The Aryans believed in many gods and goddesses. But they also believed that all the gods and goddesses were parts of one supreme force, or god, called Brahman [BRAH-mun]. Their main gods were Vishnu the Preserver and Shiva the Changer.

Eventually, the beliefs of the Aryans grew into the complex religion known as Hinduism [HIN-doo-iz-um]. This is still the major religion of India. Over the centuries, Hinduism has changed and absorbed the beliefs of many of India's peoples besides those of the Aryans. But Hinduism is rooted in an idea that dates from Aryan times: all humans are part of nature and are governed by its laws. All gods, all people, and all things are part of one universal spirit. Everything and everybody has a place in nature's order.

The Kumbh Mela [koomb MAY-luh] festival is one of the oldest in the world. Millions of people gather at the spot on the Ganges where Hindus believe the universe was created.

Ancient Mysteries

Who Was the Fertility Goddess?

We know a lot about the roots of Hinduism because the Aryans wrote down their beliefs in a religious text called the Veda. What do we know about prehistoric religions such as the one practised by the people of the Indus Valley civilization? Very little. The earliest religions were passed from parents to children by word of mouth. Wise people in some societies were assigned the task of memorizing the ancient religious stories. But nothing of the wisdom or stories of these people was written down. For this reason, prehistoric religions remain a big mystery.

We do know that religion was important to people. Some of the oldest objects ever found were used in religious rituals. Cave paintings, pottery figurines, and sites of human and animal sacrifice suggest that even the earliest humans looked to the gods for answers. Spiritual beliefs were part of everyday life.

Among the ruins of the Indus Valley cities, archaeologists found statues of a fertility goddess. Archaeologists have found similar statues scattered across much of western Asia and Europe. What do we know about the fertility goddess? Next to nothing. With no written records describing the people's beliefs, all we know for sure is that it must have been a widespread religion.

What does this fertility goddess tell you about the Indus Valley?

This artifact hints at the belief system of many prehistoric people.

A New Social Order

We've seen that Hinduism developed out of the beliefs of the Aryans. Part of that belief system says that all things have a place in nature's order. An age-old Indian social structure has its roots in that idea. According to the Aryans, it was the law of nature that people belonged to particular classes, or **castes**.

At the top of the social structure were the **Brahmins**, who were powerful priests. Brahmins were considered the most "pure" caste. Then came the nobles and warriors. Below them were merchants, shopkeepers, craftspeople, and farmers. Then came servants. At the bottom were the people who had to do the most unpleasant and unclean work. They became known as the **Untouchables** because no one was supposed to touch them. Through thousands of years, these people had no hope of improving their situation.

Over the centuries, many reformers in India have fought against the caste system, especially for the sake of the millions of people of no caste. Untouchability was banned in 1950, but in some areas of India it persists.

In its early stages, the Aryan system of caste was not hereditary. People could change their caste. For example, a warrior who wished to become a priest could do so. As time went by, the caste system became rigid. There was no way to escape the fate to which you were born.

Over the next 1000 years, the Hinduism of the Aryans became much more than a religion. Hinduism and the caste system went hand in hand as the society's basic social structure. The four original castes split up into thousands of sub-castes. Each sub-caste had a place above and below other groups. People were expected to do the jobs assigned to them and to devote their lives to elaborate rituals and offerings to the gods. Because of their supposed access to the gods, the Brahmin priests were dominant over everyone.

PERSPECTIVES

On Caste

Supporters of the caste system point to its religious importance. Others believe it is practical. Here, Indian writer Prafulla Mohanti [prah-FOOL-luh moe-HAHN-tee] explains why he believed the caste system helped his village function.

The caste system is practical. A village needs people from different castes to make it function. Society needs people to provide different services. It needs Brahmins for religious work, washermen to wash clothes, barbers to cut hair, traders, craftsmen, cleaners, etc. They all belong to different castes according to the service they provide, and together they form the village community.

Opponents of the caste system do not believe that the class system or Untouchability exist for religious reasons. They believe that this system continues because it ensures that India will always have a lot of people who will do the unpleasant jobs for little money. Untouchables have no choice but to take the dirty work. Mahatma Gandhi [muh-HAT-muh GAN-dee], the greatest religious and political leader of modern India, believed that the caste system was unjust:

… Caste has nothing to do with religion in general and Hinduism in particular. It is a sin to believe anyone else is inferior or superior to ourselves. We are all equal.

Think For Yourself

1. According to the caste system of ancient India, people were valued for what they could contribute to the group. How did this view of the individual affect life in ancient India?

2. In modern India, people are valued as individuals. As a result, Indian law forbids discrimination based on a person's caste. Think of another way that modern laws protect our rights to be individuals.

New Visions of Society

Only by trying new ways of doing things can a society meet the ever-changing needs of people.

O ver a thousand years, from about 1500 to 500 BCE, the culture of the Aryans transformed into a new civilization along the Ganges River. Great cities grew up, written language reappeared, and trade with other peoples of the ancient world flourished.

All over the ancient world, the population was growing rapidly. As the cities and towns of India grew, life became more complex. The people of India needed better ways to live together so that everyone could

contribute to and benefit from their society. They started considering new ways of doing things.

Religious Rebels

As a social structure, ancient Hinduism and the caste system helped keep order for many centuries. It enabled many people to live together peacefully. But the Indian people had progressed—they no longer needed such a rigid social structure. The people began to rebel. Religious leaders who rejected their own powerful priesthood led the search for answers.

The religious leader who was most successful in challenging the rigid system of ancient Hinduism was Siddhartha Gautama, who lived between 560 and 480 BCE. He became known as Buddha [BOO-duh], which means "the **Enlightened** One." The belief system he founded is called **Buddhism**.

Buddha was an Indian prince who gave up his riches to search for religious truth. He taught people to live simply, not wanting riches and power. He believed that people should be kind to one another and to animals.

An enlightened person is one who sees clearly, one who understands spiritual truth.

As their cities grew, the people of ancient India began to search for answers about how people should live together. The questions they asked have reappeared time and time again throughout history. For example, which of these five questions does our government struggle with when it tries to make decisions about Canada's social programs?

How can we make life good for all people?

Where will we live and work?

Why are we here on earth?

Who should be in charge?

How should we settle disagreements?

Perhaps Buddha's most revolutionary teaching was that rituals and caste were unimportant—all people were equal. In early Buddhist communities, monks of all castes lived together, made decisions together and ate at the same table. Instead of sacrificing animals to the gods, they meditated and prayed.

Buddhism is no longer a major religion in India. Nonetheless, it has had a lasting influence in India in two ways. First, many of its humane ideas became part of Hinduism. Second, it affected the way people thought, especially about the worth of individuals and the way the country should be governed.

This artifact is evidence of the spread of Buddhism into Asia.

Buddha's message of truth, **compassion** (sympathy), and care for others gained many followers as it spread eastward into Asia. Today Buddhism is a major religion throughout Asia, including Indonesia, where this Buddha sits.

Investigate

Work in a small group to research several world religions. Each student can focus on a different religion. Independently, conduct some research to answer the following questions in point form.

- Where did this religion develop?
- When did it develop?
- What are the central beliefs?
- What are the major ceremonies and festivals?
- Where do people practise it now?

Meet with your other group members. On chart paper, create a large chart that displays the group's findings. Take turns comparing the various religions and finding connections between them. Assign one person to take notes of the group's observations.

A Greek ambassador who visited the Indian city of Patna wrote about his surprise to find a well-organized government that did not rely on slave labour—unlike the government of Greece at the time.

The lion from Asoka's pillar is the emblem of modern India. Even today, Asoka is beloved for his ideas about tolerance.

A New Vision of Government

The emperor Asoka [uh-SOKE-uh] was the earliest leader to be influenced by Buddhism. He started off as a powerful military leader. He united many small states in India through a series of bloody conquests. In his final assault, in 273 BCE, he caused the deaths of more than 100 000 people. Afterwards, the suffering he had caused suddenly appalled him. He decided to end his conquests and change the ruthless way he governed.

After studying Buddhism, Asoka changed. He came to believe that common people were worthy of respect and rights. He tried to govern by using the Buddhist ideals of compassion, tolerance, and truthfulness as his guides. Asoka refused to use his power to control people's lives. Instead, he tried to rule fairly, using reason and morality as his guides. He used the wealth of the empire to improve the people's living conditions, building roads, hospitals, rest houses, and irrigation projects.

Asoka united the many different people in his empire by promoting religious tolerance and respect for all living things. He taught people about how to live the "right way." He had his beliefs carved on stone pillars and on the walls of caves so that people would come across them on their travels.

Asoka built pillars in grounds like this around India to get his message to ordinary people. Why do you think he put one in this particular location?

This artifact marks the site of Buddha's first sermon.

Think For Yourself

Both Buddha and Asoka worked hard to find the "right way." Buddha developed a new religion that encouraged people to find enlightenment by "right views" and "right efforts." Asoka ruled with tolerance, and encouraged people to live the "right way." In your notebook or social studies journal, describe what "living the right way" is for you personally.

Looking Back

In this chapter, you have seen how the Indus Valley civilization flourished but finally disappeared. You also learned about the Indian civilization that developed, changed over time, and survived until modern times. What characteristic of Indian civilization do you think allowed it to survive?

Chapter 7

China:
A World to Itself

f you had to get a message to someone in China, how would you send it? Maybe you would pick up the telephone, write an e-mail, or send a fax. Or you might write a letter that would travel by air, ship, truck, or train. You could even jump on a plane and deliver your message in person.

In the ancient world, none of these possibilities existed. Travelling on a horse, by boat, or on foot, you might have been able to deliver a message to a nearby neighbour—but certainly not to ancient China. Since prehistoric times, the Chinese have been isolated from their distant neighbours by vast oceans, deserts, and mountain ranges. The ancient Chinese knew nothing about the rest of the world, and the rest of the world knew nothing about ancient China.

In this chapter you can learn about China—the oldest continuing civilization to arise apart from the rest of the world. You'll learn how ancient China's independence helped it become a world unto itself.

The Middle Kingdom

China is home to the first great civilization of eastern Asia and one of the oldest civilizations in the world. Much of the ancient Chinese way of life has survived through times of prosperity and poverty, and through times of war and peace. In China we see a rare thing: a culture with roots in prehistoric times that has survived to the present day.

But why did such a long-lasting civilization arise in eastern Asia? As you've seen before, the character of the land plays an important role. First of all, China is large—very large. Today, China is the third largest country in area, after Russia and Canada. Second, much of the land—15 per cent—was fertile, so the people could grow enough food for a large population. Today, China has the largest population of any country. This was probably true in ancient times as well. Third, mountains, jungles, and oceans surrounded and protected the new civilization.

The ancient Chinese believed that their land was the centre of the world. Their own name for China—the **Middle Kingdom**—tells us how they saw themselves.

Today China is home to 1.2 billion people. Canada's population could fit into China's 40 times.

This artifact shows how people carried water.

China has some of the world's largest cities, but most people still live in the countryside. Compare the ancient Chinese painting, shown at left, with the photograph taken in China recently. How do they show that the Chinese have passed on culture from one generation to another.

A Protected Land

The geography of East Asia set it apart from the rest of the world. Where it wasn't bordered by ocean, it was cut off by mountains and deserts. These **natural barriers** created a closed world, where the growing population was safe from invaders. Because it was left untouched by outside influences, the early settlements of ancient China grew into a great civilization different from any other.

What specific geographic features can you find on this map that would have protected ancient China from invasion? The horse-riding people of the steppes, known as Mongolians, caused a great deal of destruction. Look on the map to find what the ancient Chinese built to protect themselves.

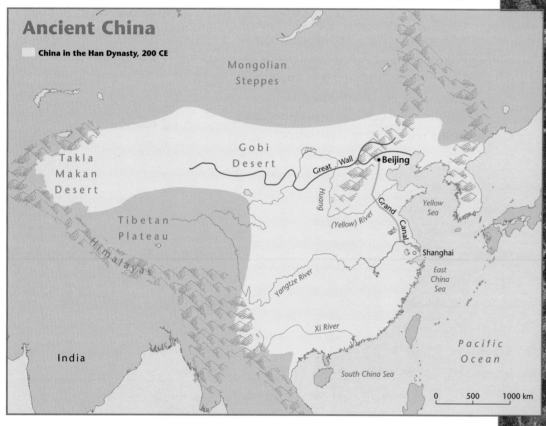

Ancient China

China in the Han Dynasty, 200 CE

Mongolian Steppes

Takla Makan Desert

Gobi Desert

Great Wall

Beijing

Huang (Yellow) River

Grand Canal

Yellow Sea

Tibetan Plateau

Himalayas

Yangtze River

Shanghai

East China Sea

India

Xi River

Pacific Ocean

South China Sea

0   500   1000 km

China's Great Wall stretches 2250 km. It is the only structure made by humans that can be seen from outer space. This space radar image was taken from the space shuttle. Imagine that Canada built a 2250-km wall along the Canada–United States border, starting at the Pacific Ocean. Check on a map of Canada to find out in what province it would end.

Crucial Waterways

Like many ancient people, the early Chinese first settled along riverbanks.

The Huang [HWONG] River (also known as the Yellow River) was the site of ancient China's first cities. The river flowed through the rich, yellow soil of China's central plain, where it picked up a huge amount of yellow silt, called **loess** [LOH-es]. It carried this precious cargo along its length to the valleys downstream. Although the people valued the Huang River, they also knew its destructive power. Its floods had ruined so many crops and drowned so many villagers, that the people nicknamed it "China's Sorrow."

The Yangtze [YANK-tsee] River is even longer than the Huang. At 4800 km, it is the third-longest river in the world. Growing rice plants require a lot of water. The low-lying Yangtze Delta, with its plentiful water, provided the perfect rice-growing environment. Half of China's crops are now grown in the Yangtze Delta.

About 2500 years ago, the ancient Chinese began building canals to link their great rivers. Eventually, the rivers and canals formed a network of waterways. Food could be moved through this network to people living on barren lands. People could send grain by boat to pay their taxes. The emperor's armies could travel quickly to trouble spots. Further, the waterways served as a network of highways, allowing people to travel fairly easily to visit distant family and friends. For ordinary people, the waterways encouraged a strong sense of belonging to a larger society.

The Grand Canal joined four river systems and stretched 1600 km from north to south. Today it still carries boats transporting grain, coal, lumber, cotton, and manufactured goods.

About 85 per cent of China is mountain or desert. The early population clustered on the 15 per cent that was good for farming. What advantages does this river site offer a farmer?

Try This

On the map of China on page 132 find the following: Gobi Desert, Himalayas, Takla Makan Desert, the Great Wall, Huang River, Yangtze River, and the Pacific Ocean.

- Make a list of these features and places.

- Beside each, describe how it made ancient China suitable for civilization to emerge, or how it protected ancient China from outside influences.

- Write a summarizing paragraph explaining how environmental factors influenced the development of Chinese civilization.

PERSPECTIVES

Deciding a River's Fate

What would happen if you destroyed part of a river? That's a question many Chinese people are asking now. The Chinese government is building the Three Gorges Dam across the Yangtze River. It promises to be the world's largest dam. The goal is to tap the river's waterpower to make electricity. People disagree about whether the dam will be a great step forwards or the most destructive creation in history. Here are some of the reasons each side gives for its position.

For the Dam

- *The dam will supply the energy China needs for new businesses and factories.*

- *China will decrease the amount of coal it burns. This will lessen air pollution and health problems caused by burning coal.*

- *The costs of getting around on the river will decrease.*

- *The dam will control flooding along the river. This constant threat has cost hundreds of thousands of lives in the last hundred years alone.*

Against the Dam

- *The dam will cost too much, about a billion dollars. Ordinary Chinese people will have to pay higher taxes and lose services that their tax money would otherwise buy.*

- *More than a million people will have to move from their homes to cities, where work and housing are hard to find.*

- *A giant 1000-km² lake behind the dam will cover hundreds of villages, factories, important historic sites, and the habitat of birds and animals.*

- *No one knows for sure how the dam will stand up to earthquakes.*

This dam is a good example of a large-scale project that carries many benefits and many costs. Communities all over the world face similar dilemmas and have to answer the same question: How should we balance the effects of our choices so that we ensure the best possible future for everyone? It's a tough question.

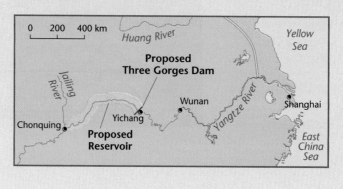

Think For Yourself

Work with a partner to come up with a position on whether the promised benefits of the Three Gorges Dam outweigh the likely costs. To help you weigh the effects of the dam, list the pros and cons given above. Beside each one, answer this question: "Whose lives will be improved and whose will be made worse?"

Review your list to reach a position. What problems would still have to be solved? With your partner, explain your position to another pair of students.

Life in Ancient China

What was life like in a civilization isolated from the rest of the ancient world? Surprisingly, it was a lot like life in other ancient civilizations. The people were able to produce a surplus of food from the rich land. With that advantage, great developments followed. Thriving cities grew up in which the arts, trade, technology, and education blossomed. The people developed a written language, a system of government, and laws. Over time, a carefully ordered society emerged that grew steadily in size, wealth, and power, and eventually became the most influential civilization of Asia.

A Layered Society

Like other civilizations, ancient China was unified by a social structure in which everyone had a place. The social structure was like a ladder, each group in society belonging on one rung. People were free to move up the ladder, but only a lucky few ever did.

The social structure of ancient China offered a unique opportunity for people to improve their social standing: If people—even the poorest people—could pass a special set of examinations, they could become civil servants.

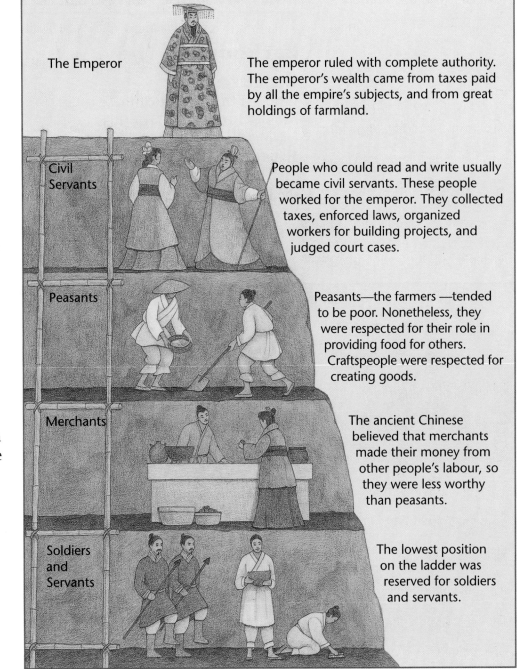

The Emperor

The emperor ruled with complete authority. The emperor's wealth came from taxes paid by all the empire's subjects, and from great holdings of farmland.

Civil Servants

People who could read and write usually became civil servants. These people worked for the emperor. They collected taxes, enforced laws, organized workers for building projects, and judged court cases.

Peasants

Peasants—the farmers —tended to be poor. Nonetheless, they were respected for their role in providing food for others. Craftspeople were respected for creating goods.

Merchants

The ancient Chinese believed that merchants made their money from other people's labour, so they were less worthy than peasants.

Soldiers and Servants

The lowest position on the ladder was reserved for soldiers and servants.

Make a chart with headings for the different social structures you've learned about (Egypt, page 101; India, page 124; and ancient China, page 135). For each civilization, rank the social layers, from most to least powerful.

a) What similarities do you see in the way that ancient societies were structured? What differences can you find?

b) About 90 per cent of ancient peoples were peasants. Which civilization would you have wanted to live in as a peasant? Be sure to give reasons for your choice.

Although the practice of slavery did exist in ancient China, it was uncommon.

One of the hardest farm tasks was controlling the supply of water to the fields. Farmers carried water by bucket or used irrigation machines. In this photograph, farmers transplant seedlings into water-covered fields, just as peasants did 3000 years ago.

Backbone of the Culture

Who fed the ancient Chinese people? Farmers did. For this reason, the ancient Chinese were grateful to farming people, and gave them a special place in their society. Since ancient times, farmers have been considered the backbone of the culture.

Nonetheless, ancient farmers lived a simple life. They farmed small plots of land, which they owned. With the produce of their land, peasants could feed themselves and pay their taxes but not much else. Their one-room huts had earthen floors and little furniture.

The work of rice farmers was hard and unending. Few animals were available to help, so people did all the work themselves. Everyone in a farming family worked in the fields. Women and men worked together, and children pitched in when necessary. For example, after the rice seedlings grew, they had to be **transplanted**, or moved, quickly.

Harvest was another time of intensive work. If the crop failed or could not be harvested in time, the whole family faced ruin. Without a good harvest, farmers would not have enough grain to pay their taxes and still have enough left over to feed themselves all year. The poorest peasants sometimes sold themselves or their children into slavery.

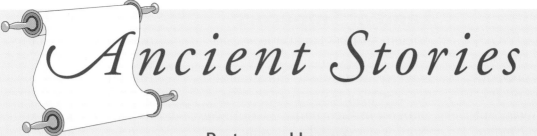

Ancient Stories

Return Home

Even though farming was hard work, the peasants' simple life was considered an ideal way to live. The ancient Chinese poet Tao Yuanming [TOH yoo-MING] had to leave his poor family of farmers to become a government official in a nearby city. After several years, he decided to return to the simple life of a farmer. In this poem he describes his thoughts while travelling home.

My fields and garden will be covered with weeds;
Why not return? …
My boat lightly tosses on the broad waters;
The wind, whirling, blows my robe about …
Then I espy my humble house;
So I am glad, so I run …
Riches and honour are not my desire …
I desire a fair morning to go out alone;
Sometimes to plant my staff and weed or hoe;

Or climb the eastern hill and let out long whistles;
Or looking on the clear stream, compose a poem.
So following change, I shall go to my end;
Happy in my destiny, why should I doubt any more?

Excerpt from Tao Yuanming, "Return Home," from Ian McGreal (ed.), *Great Literature of the Eastern World*, (New York: HarperCollins, 1996), p. 59

Chinese artwork often shows peaceful scenes from nature. This painting shows a grasshopper on a snow-pea plant. What values does this picture or the poem illustrate to you?

China: A World to Itself | **137**

The Empress Wu [WOO] was China's first and only woman ruler. This powerful leader murdered most of her political rivals, but she also improved Chinese society. For example, she allowed women into the civil service, encouraged agriculture, and reduced taxes.

Land of Emperors

Ancient China's backbone was its farmers, but its head was the emperor. You can see the ancient Chinese people's respect for the emperor in their name for him: the "Son of Heaven." The people believed that the emperor had authority because heaven had given him the task of ruling ancient China; he had the **"Mandate of Heaven."** The emperor had a heavenly duty to take care of the Chinese people. In turn, citizens had a duty to be obedient and loyal to the emperor. As a result of this bargain, the emperors enjoyed great power and wealth, and had a great influence on their subjects' lives.

The people did have one way of making sure the emperor tried to be a good ruler. If the emperor did not rule fairly, the people could decide that their ruler had lost the mandate of heaven. When that happened, the peasants were freed of their obligation to obey. Usually a rebellion would result—the emperor would be overthrown, and a new **dynasty** would gain power.

When a series of emperors all come from the same family, we call them a dynasty. Some Chinese dynasties lasted for hundreds of years, and had dozens of emperors. The last dynasty ended in 1912 when the emperor was overthrown at the age of six.

Qin Shihuangdi [CHIN shee-hwong-DEE] was the first ruler of ancient China to call himself "emperor." He founded the Qin Dynasty, which gave China its name. Though he ruled for only 15 years, he had a great influence on Chinese civilization.

Shang [SHANG] 1766–1122 BCE	• This is China's first dynasty of emperors. • They create a great Bronze Age culture. • Chinese writing develops. • Horse-drawn chariots appear.	
Zhou [JOW] 1122–256 BCE	• These emperors organize China into a **feudal system.** • They start many large-scale public works. • They introduce the use of iron for agricultural tools and military weapons.	In a feudal [FYOOD-ul] system, peasants pay rent to a lord for the right to farm the land.
Qin [CHIN] 221–206 BCE	• The first emperor unites China. • He standardizes weights and measures. • He standardizes laws and taxes all over the empire. • A strong, central rule begins that will last 2000 years. • He builds the first sections of the Great Wall.	
Han [HAN] 202 BCE–220 CE	• These emperors create the national civil service. • Paper is invented. • Great scientific discoveries and inventions appear.	Four dynasties ruled China during ancient times. Each left a lasting influence on the future civilization of China. This chart summarizes the main features of these early dynasties.

Investigate

Work in a group of four to create a time line of China's ancient period.

• First, decide on one dynasty for each group member to research.

• Find out the main achievements of your dynasty, and the dates when they happened. (To help you research, see the How To Research Feature on pages 3–4.)

• With your partners, create a time line for the period 2000 BCE to 500 CE. Mark each important date and achievement on the time line.

• Take turns presenting the highlights of your chosen dynasty to your group.

Ancient Mysteries

The Terra Cotta Soldiers

In 1974, a group of Chinese farmers were digging a well when they came upon a spectacular archaeological find. As the ground fell away, they saw the first of an army of life-sized clay soldiers—a total of 7000, each with a different face.

The **terra cotta** (red clay) army, as the clay soldiers are known, are a mystery to archaeologists. What message were they supposed to send, and to whom? Were these clay soldiers meant to come to life somehow? And why were they buried here?

The clue that provides some answers is an enormous mound lying about 1.5 km away. This mound contains the tomb of Emperor Qin Shihuangdi, the first ruler of China to take the name of emperor. The tomb has never been opened, but an ancient historian wrote about it a hundred years after the emperor's death, around 200 BCE. He described a dazzling complex that took 700 000 workers almost 36 years to build. The tomb was built as a labyrinth, with huge pits, blind alleys, and crossbows set to fire on anyone who dared to enter the tomb after it was sealed. Inside, miniature versions of China's rivers, made of mercury, flowed into a tiny ocean. The emperor's childless wives were buried with him. So were the craftspeople who built the tomb. That way, the tomb's secrets could never be revealed.

The ancient historian who described Qin Shihuangdi's tomb said nothing about the terra cotta warriors, though they were created around the same time. Were they set in place to guard the emperor's tomb for eternity? Or did they have some other purpose, perhaps to defend the city from attack, as most experts believe? But how would clay soldiers do that? Perhaps we'll find out more if Qin Shihuangdi's tomb is ever opened.

The terra cotta army includes 7000 large-as-life soldiers, with horses and real weapons. Every soldier looks different. If you look at the photograph here and on the cover of this book, you will see how lifelike and serene they look.

These artifacts show the power of the emperor.

PERSPECTIVES

Great Ruler vs. Ruthless Tyrant

Historians still don't agree if Qin Shihuangdi, the first emperor, was a great ruler or a cruel, oppressive tyrant.

The Great Ruler

On the one hand, historians admire Qin Shihuangdi because he accomplished what many had tried and failed to do: he unified the many warring states in ancient China into a single state with a central government. His system of government lasted for 2000 years. He also ended **feudalism** in ancient China. Under feudalism, rich lords had ruled over all the people who worked under them. Qin Shihuangdi built a network of roads and canals across ancient China and began building the Great Wall. He standardized laws, the writing system, money, weights, and measures. He even ordered that all carts be built to the same width so that their wheels would create ruts that all carts could travel in.

The Ruthless Tyrant

On the other hand, Qin Shihuangdi is remembered for many harsh and unjust actions. He ordered the burning of all books as a way to destroy any ideas he didn't like. He even buried live historians along with their books. He forced people to work on his great projects, where many thousands died. On the building of the Great Wall, he buried groups of workers alive to scare the others into working harder. He forced people to build roads not for the good of the people but so that his soldiers could collect taxes more easily.

Think For Yourself

With a partner, discuss the following statements:

- "Ancient rulers like Qin Shihuangdi should be remembered for their great works. The benefits they brought to people's lives outweighed the costs."

- "Ancient rulers like Qin Shihuangdi should not be remembered for their great works, because it was ordinary people who built them. The cost to ordinary people outweighed the benefits."

1. Decide if you agree with one statement or the other. Give at least two reasons for your position. Alternatively, write a new statement that gives your own opinion on how ancient rulers should be remembered.

2. As times change and the values of society evolve, we want different qualities in our leaders. Identify three qualities that you think a great leader in modern Canada should have. Would you expect a leader in ancient times to have these qualities? Why, or why not?

Harmony Between Earth and Heaven

Have you ever seen the symbol above? Since ancient times, the Chinese have used it to show the two opposite forces of nature: yin and yang. The strength of this idea is proven in its survival through thousands of years.

When a person died in ancient China, everyone believed that the person's spirit lived on in the afterworld. People thought that their ancestors had magical powers for punishing them or helping them make wise decisions.

To keep their ancestors happy, the ancient Chinese built altars for them in and outside their homes. Here a modern family keeps its altar outside. What does this practice say about the ancient Chinese?

The Chinese culture is very ancient, with roots in prehistory. From very early times, the Chinese understood that they could survive only if they lived in harmony with nature. The ancient Chinese believed that harmony in the universe depended on a balance between the forces of nature called "yin" and "yang." Yin and yang are the opposites in life: dark and light, heat and cold, female and male, and many others.

All people were expected to try to find balance between the forces of nature in their everyday lives. People believed that the destructive forces of nature—floods, earthquakes, and droughts—were sent as punishments when the people were not living in harmony with the earth.

Family

The ancient Chinese saw the family as the source of harmony. For rich and poor alike, the family was of first importance. If one member of a family did something wrong, the entire family was in disgrace. If one member excelled, he or she brought honour to everyone. This dependence on one another encouraged everyone to try hard.

The ideal ancient Chinese family was large, with many

generations living together in one household. The oldest male was considered the head of the family. Women, whether rich or poor, were expected to be gentle and to respect their husbands. They maintained their homes, worked in the fields, and looked after their children and grandchildren.

The ancient Chinese believed that children had a responsibility to continue the good name of their families. They were expected to obey their parents without a fuss because respect for elders was their duty. Children, of course, could look forward to the time when their own children would honour them, both as elders, and finally as ancestors.

Three Ways

During a long period of warfare (400–200 BCE), the ancient Chinese began to search for a way to live that would bring peace and harmony back to the empire. They found three different systems of beliefs: **Confucianism** [kun-FYOO-shuh-niz-um], **Taoism** [TOW-iz-um], and, much later, Buddhism. All three **philosophies** became popular, although they were very different. People combined their new beliefs with the older beliefs in nature spirits and, ancestor worship. In time, the ancient Chinese came to see the three ways of thinking as the "three ways to one goal." All three philosophies continue to be important to the Chinese people today.

Confucius tried to help ancient China build a just and stable society by using common sense. He believed that if people developed what he called "moral virtue," or plain

goodness, they could govern themselves.

Laozi [low-TSAY], the founder of Taoism, lived about the same time as Confucius but had a very different view of life. He believed that people should follow the Tao, or "way," by living simple lives that are as much in harmony with nature as possible. Laozi said, "A thousand-mile journey begins with a single step."

Both Confucianism and Taoism affected the way Chinese people approached life. Buddhism reached China from India in the first century CE, about 600 years after Confucius and Laozi had lived. Buddhism, although it came later, eventually became the most widely practised religion in China. Chinese Buddhism differs from Indian Buddhism. In China, for example, the popular Buddhist figure called Guanyin [kwon-YIN] appeared as female rather than male.

A good person is one "who loves others. The good person wishing to stand himself helps others to stand; wishing to arrive, helps others arrive. The ability to see the parallel to your own case is the secret of goodness." – *Confucius*

A philosophy is a set of beliefs resulting from a search for truth, or knowledge about the nature of the universe.

Confucius's most important teaching was that people should respect one another. Parents should respect their children, and children should honour their parents. Similarly, rulers should respect their subjects, and subjects should honour their rulers.

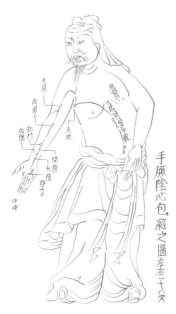

Acupuncture is an ancient Chinese technique for mending the body. It stimulates the body's *qi*, which means "life energy."

The Chinese year has many festivals that date back to ancient times. In this picture, Chinese Canadians celebrate the Chinese New Year in Vancouver. This festival dates back to ancient times, when farmers celebrated the new growing season and prayed for good crops.

Finding the Past in the Present

The Chinese have preserved many of their ways for thousands of years. For example, the Chinese have a tradition of making beautiful objects from bronze, jade, silk, and **porcelain** [POR-suh-lin] (a fine ceramic). Much of the ancient artistic methods, styles, and images have survived.

The ancient Chinese civilization can be seen everywhere in the modern world—in China and in other countries. For example, today people around the world enjoy cooking and eating Chinese food. Delicious food and good company have made life pleasant for the Chinese people since ancient times. By using herbs and spices, even poor people could transform their diet of rice and vegetables into a celebration of flavour. The ancient Chinese technique of stir-frying is fast, so it uses little fuel and preserves the food's natural flavour and nutrients.

Investigate

Find and bring to class a Chinese cultural artifact or a picture or illustration of one. Present it to a small group, explaining its connection to ancient Chinese culture.

East Meets West

During the Han Dynasty, from around 200 BCE to 200 CE, the Chinese Empire grew in power. It gradually brought more and more independent Asian lands under its control, and ancient Chinese civilization spread into these new territories. China gained access to new goods and new trading partners. China's armies guarded their territories and fought off invaders. They also made it safe for traders to travel within the empire.

Throughout the ancient world, other civilizations were experiencing the same kind of growth. As populations grew, new lands were settled. People discovered new neighbours. Sometimes this led to conflict as peoples battled for control of precious resources. But other contacts were beneficial.

Despite the mountains and oceans that separated ancient China from the rest of the world, rumours of the great riches of the Chinese Empire eventually spread to the people outside China's borders. Rome, the great empire of the Western world, heard about ancient China and its fabled riches. If it could trade with ancient China, Rome would gain luxuries never seen before in the Western world.

Although the ancient Chinese heard about Rome, they weren't particularly interested. After all, what could people from foreign lands offer the Chinese? Ancient China was a **self-sufficient** society in every way—the Chinese had everything they needed. Their cities were carefully structured so that they could feed their large populations. They had art, music, theatre, and beautiful buildings. Through the influence of the three Chinese philosophies, ancient China had a stable society. People performed their duty according to their place in society, and the society ran well.

The ancient Chinese thought of the people who lived outside their borders as uncivilized and uncultured.

These trucks still travel along the ancient trade route known as the Silk Road. The weather along the Silk Road can be cold and snowy in winter, and blistering hot and dry in summer. Some of the roads cling to mountainsides, so landslides are still a danger.

The Silk Road

The Romans wanted the Chinese silk they'd heard about. In return, they offered horses, gold, jade, ivory, furs, glass, metals, and muslin. Eventually these goods tempted the ancient Chinese, and trade began between the West and the East. Across thousands of miles of mountain, desert, and plain, traders led camel caravans loaded with precious goods. Because the route was long and treacherous, traders usually worked only one section of the route. Goods passed from trader to trader until they reached their final destination. These trade links between settlements eventually grew into a great chain joining East and West: the **Silk Road**.

Silk from China was one of the most valuable goods of the ancient world. Compared with the fabrics of cotton, linen, and wool that other early peoples had, silk was light and fine—a cloth of remarkable beauty. Although silk was what the Romans craved, the ancient Chinese were soon supplying them with porcelain, spices, tea, and seemingly exotic flowers and fruits such as roses and oranges.

The ancient Chinese carefully guarded the secret of silk making so that no one else could make it. How would anyone guess that worms found in China's mulberry bushes spun the fine threads? Even the Chinese had come upon the discovery by accident. According to legend, the 14-year-old wife of one of the emperors of ancient China began unravelling a long, white thread from a worm cocoon that she had accidentally dropped into her teacup!

Traders travelled the Silk Road for over 1600 years. During that time it was never known as the Silk Road. A German explorer gave it that name about 100 years ago.

People in much of the ancient world took part in the trading networks that developed through Europe and Asia. Explorers, religious seekers, and ambassadors also travelled the trade routes. Why do you think the great armies of the Chinese and Roman Empires worked so hard to keep the routes open?

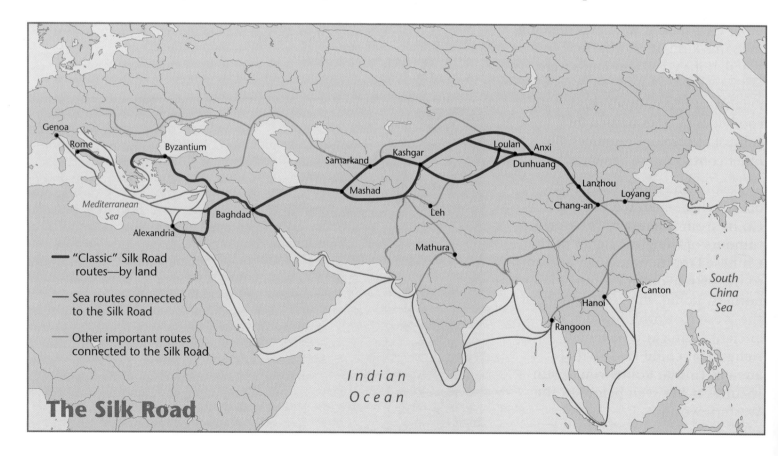

The Silk Road

— "Classic" Silk Road routes—by land

— Sea routes connected to the Silk Road

— Other important routes connected to the Silk Road

Try This

1. In a small group, choose one of the trading routes shown on the map of the Silk Road. Imagine you are a company of traders preparing to take a caravan of camels along your chosen route. Do some research so you can make a plan for the trip.

   - Draw a map of your route.

   - Who will you trade with?

   - What will you trade?

   - Choose the time of year you will travel. Justify your choice.

   - List the supplies you will bring with you. Remember to consider the features of the land and the climate.

2. Now imagine that you have made your trip. On your own, write three excerpts from a journal you kept on your imaginary trip. Read the feature on How to Write a Fictional Travel Journal for tips.

Precipitation	
	over 400 mm
	250 mm – 400 mm
	150 mm – 250 mm
	50 mm – 150 mm
	25 mm – 50 mm
	under 25 mm

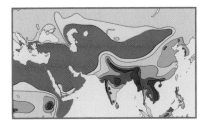

This map, or one showing temperatures, can help you plan your trip. So can a map showing natural features such as mountains and deserts.

HOW TO... Write a Fictional Travel Journal

To write a fictional travel journal, you have to put yourself in the place of a traveller. If you want your travel diary to seem realistic, you need both facts and imagination.

Want to get to know the route you took? → Find an atlas with detailed maps.

Want to know if you were comfortable? → Research the climate of the area.

Want to write about realistic events? → Find out what historical events took place at the time. Find out what religious festivals were popular. Note any geographical features that would have inspired you with awe on your first sighting of them.

Want to give your journal authentic detail? → Describe your surroundings, the weather, the homes, and the route. You can even add sketches.

Want to add a personal touch? → Include your thoughts about home: how long you were away, what comforts you missed, and who you missed. Mention what you looked forward to doing or seeing next.

Want to keep your readers interested? → Mention incidents that occurred on your trip, such as problems you had or interesting people you met.

Want to make your diary seem realistic? → Include the gritty details: how and what you ate, where you went to the bathroom, how and where you slept, and how often you bathed.

The Origins of the Silk Road

For many centuries, the Chinese had only small, pony-like horses. One of the ancient emperors, Han Wudi [HAN woo-DEE] (140–87 BCE), heard stories that large, powerful horses could be found in the mountains far to the west, beyond China's borders. These "heavenly horses," as the Chinese called them, would be strong enough to carry warriors in armour into battle.

Han Wudi sent an expedition of 100 men to bring back some of the heavenly horses. The journey across the baking desert and over the high mountain passes was an almost impossible mission. Only one man survived, and he spent over 10 years as a prisoner of unfriendly people. But 13 years after leaving home, he finally returned to China. He did not bring back horses, but he did tell the emperor that the rumours were true: The horses were as impressive as the emperor had heard. The traveller also reported that two great empires lay beyond the mountains: India and Persia.

On receiving the news, the emperor sent another expedition in search of the horses. But the breeders refused to sell their horses. When the expedition returned empty-handed, the emperor sent an army of 60 000. The mission succeeded in capturing a herd of horses and bringing them to China. It also spread Chinese control along a 2400-km route that would eventually become the main route of the Silk Road.

Both goods, such as this bronze horse, and ideas spread slowly but steadily in the ancient world. People wrote, talked, travelled, and traded. Each contact expanded the web of connections among people.

Trading Ideas

Trade between East and West brought the participating countries new riches in manufactured goods and raw materials. More important, they gained new ideas, beliefs, scientific knowledge, and technologies. This spread of knowledge was to have far more influence than the benefits brought by a few luxury goods.

The ancient Chinese valued the skills of reading and writing. Because they had a strong educational system, and encouraged the exploration of new technology, the ancient Chinese came up with many creative and useful inventions. And because China developed independently, many of the technologies they invented were quite different from those invented in the West.

For example, the Chinese invented paper while people in Europe were still using **vellum** [VEL-um] (dried calfskin) and papyrus. The Chinese made paper by pounding bark, rags, and plant fibres into a pulp, which they then pressed and dried. Early paper was coated with glue to keep it from falling apart. How is paper an improvement over clay tablets or vellum?

Only through knowledge can societies grow and become more complex.

Many of the inventions of the ancient Chinese were **revolutionary** [rev-uh-LOO-shuh-nair-ee]—they changed life forever. Just think how three of them—paper, gunpowder, and the compass—have changed people's lives over the centuries.

The ancient Chinese invented the first compasses. Here you can see how different a Chinese compass looks from a Western compass. How was the compass an improvement for sailors, who previously had to sail within sight of land?

The ancient Chinese were the most advanced astronomers of the ancient world. They were the first to establish the length of a year as 365 1/4 days. The ancient Chinese were also very practical, inventing and using the wheelbarrow almost 1300 years before other countries learned of this ingenious invention.

The next time you write on paper, use a compass to find your way, or use a wheelbarrow to move dirt, thank the ancient Chinese. They were the first to come up with these and many other great ideas.

Try This

1. The list of ancient Chinese inventions is a long one. Here are a few to add to the ones mentioned on the previous page: the umbrella, the kite, playing cards, paper money, the first seismograph (for measuring earthquakes), bellows, cast iron, mechanical clocks, and guns.

   Create an advertisement describing the features of one invention of the ancient Chinese. Try to get across how this invention changed people's lives.

2. Use the information about China and the other ancient civilizations you've learned about to make a list of the ways ancient peoples communicated. Now make a list of the ways we communicate today.

   a) What are the biggest differences between the ways people communicated then and now?

   b) Look at each of your lists and describe how ancient and modern ways of communicating affect these things:

   • how people learn about new discoveries

   • how people buy and sell goods

   • daily life

Looking Back

In this chapter, you've learned how China developed as a world unto itself. Ancient China's isolation allowed it to develop a unique civilization and culture. In your opinion, what are the benefits and drawbacks of developing independently?

Greece: Searching for the Good Life

What's your definition of "the good life"? Having pizza and cold drinks while you watch a movie with your friends? An ancient Greek could probably relate.

Ancient Greeks loved the good life. They went to the theatre with friends, read entertaining poetry, and relaxed with a good meal. They especially enjoyed the freedom to do as they pleased. So they began a remarkable experiment. They created revolutionary laws, literature, and political systems. They gave people new rights and freedoms. They gave the individual dignity.

The ancient Greek civilization lasted for only a few centuries, but its efforts to make life easy and more enjoyable for individuals have been admired and imitated ever since. In this chapter, you will see why the ancient Greek way of life still stands—more than 2500 years later—as a model for achieving the good life.

Land of the Sea

The land of ancient Greece was tiny. Look at the map inside the front cover of this book, and you will see how small it was compared with the lands of other ancient civilizations.

Ancient Greek civilization developed in the southern tip of the Baltic Peninsula and on the many Greek islands dotting the Aegean Sea—a total area only about twice the size of Vancouver Island. The Greek lands are rugged and mountainous with few rivers and little rainfall. The only good farmland lies in small pockets nestled in valleys and on islands.

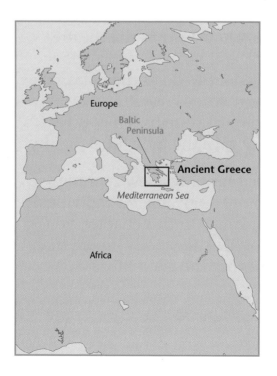

Greece's earliest settlers—northern people—enjoyed Greece's warm, dry climate. They found the hilly country to be ideal for raising sheep and goats. And crops grew easily on the small patches of farmland. These crops included grains, olives, and grapes.

The Greek lands were rich in **natural resources**. The early settlers found plenty of timber and stone for building. They also found copper, silver, obsidian, and tin. The ancient Greeks used these valuable materials for making tools and for trading with other societies. Greece's best geographic asset, however, was its seacoast. Its many natural harbours provided protection for boats, and access to a plentiful fishery.

A Civilization of City-States

Because farmland was limited to isolated pockets in Greece's mountainous lands, the earliest Greek settlements developed as small, independent communities cut off from one another. Each independent city had a **hinterland**—the surrounding farmland that provided the city with food. Each had access to the sea. Each had everything required to

---

Natural resources are materials found in nature that humans can put to use.

A Mediterranean climate is a climate made milder by a large body of water. In winter, the warmth from the water keeps the harshest weather away. In summer, cool breezes refresh the land.

Greece was home to the first civilization in Europe. It had a warm, dry, **Mediterranean** [me-dih-tuh-RAY-nee-un] **climate**, access to the sea, and pockets of fertile farmland. These conditions set the stage for a wealthy, well-organized society. Locate another place on this map that offers the same conditions.

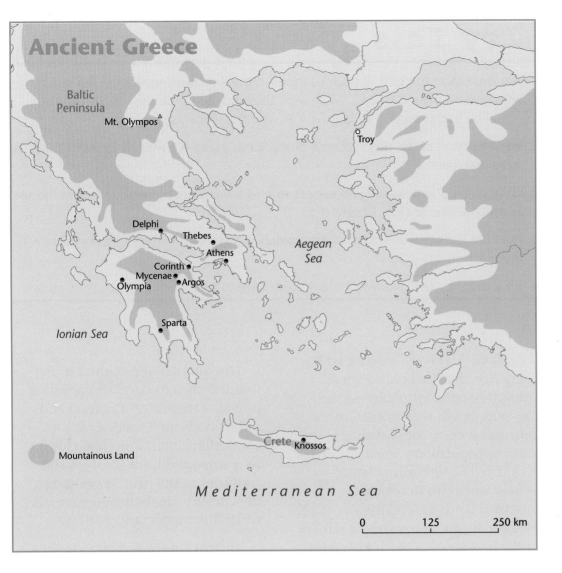

Ancient Greece

Baltic Peninsula

Mt. Olympos

Troy

Delphi

Thebes

Athens

Aegean Sea

Corinth

Mycenae
Argos

Olympia

Ionian Sea

Sparta

Mountainous Land

Crete
Knossos

Mediterranean Sea

0   125   250 km

By building trading ships, the ancient Greeks could trade with each other as well as the other communities on the Mediterranean Sea. The sea also acted as a barrier between the Greek islands and powerful neighbours. How would Greece's isolated sea location have been a disadvantage?

function as a mini-country: its own government, its own laws, and its own army. These self-governing cities are called **city-states**.

The main Greek city-states were Athens [ATH-enz], Sparta [SPAR-tuh], Corinth, Delphi [DEL-fee], Olympia [uh-LIMP-ee-uh], and Argos [AR-gos]. You can find these on the map above. At the height of ancient Greece's civilization, Athens and Sparta were the largest and most influential city-states. Many smaller ones existed, as well. Travel and communication between city-states were difficult.

Why do we talk about ancient Greece as one civilization when it was really just a collection of mini-countries? The connection was in the culture. Even though the Greek people were loyal to their own city-state, the Greek customs and traditions were shared by all. All ancient Greeks worshipped the same gods, and spoke the same language. All Greeks shared an ancestry and a way of life, so they felt a strong bond despite their individual differences. Though the various city-states sometimes fought each other, they also banded together for protection.

The ancient Greeks called themselves "Hellenes" [HEL-eenz] and their country "Hellas" [HEL-os]. It was the Romans who called them "Greek." The ancient Greeks called all people who were not Greek **barbarians** [bar-BAIR-ee-unz], which means "foreigners." The term came to mean "uncultured people."

Try This

When we look at the past, we see patterns in the way landforms and climate affected where people settled, what work they did, and how they lived. Use the information in this section to help you answer the following questions.

1. What features of the physical environment of Greece were advantages and which were drawbacks?

2. What occupations would you expect to find among people who relied on the sea as much as the ancient Greeks did?

3. How did the physical environment influence travel and communication between the different city-states?

4. How did the physical environment contribute to the development of city-states?

Traders and Warriors

Every city-state had only a small amount of good farmland. As the city-states grew, they needed more land and food to support their growing populations. Some city-states conquered neighbouring lands. Others sent ships in search of unsettled lands around the Mediterranean. Many Greeks settled in the best spots to begin **colonies** [KOL-uh-neez]. Colonies are distant settlements under the political control of a colonizing nation, in this case a city-state. The new settlements were able to raise enough food that they could feed themselves and use their surplus crops to trade with their ruling city-state.

The colonies and trading routes that the ancient Greeks established provided them with the food and other goods they needed for a comfortable life. Grain and cloth were imported from colonies and countries to the east. In exchange, the ancient Greeks traded olive oil, wine, fine metals, and pottery.

Ancient Greece was only one of a number of early seagoing cultures that grew up around the Mediterranean. The peoples living around this great sea traded, formed partnerships, and exchanged knowledge. But they also fought each other for the same valuable resources in long and destructive wars.

The Romans gave the Mediterranean its name, which means "the sea in the centre of the world." What does this tell you about the importance of the Mediterranean to the early southern Europeans?

Investigate

Conflicts between nations or city-states can have enormous consequences. For example, they can end peaceful trade, kill thousands, and destroy cultures. Read about one of the following important wars of the ancient Greeks:

- The Trojan War
- The Persian Wars
- The Peloponnesian [pel-uh-puh-NEE-zhun] War
- The Campaign of Alexander the Great

Use your research to write a newspaper article about the conflict. Your article should answer the questions What? Who? Where? When? Why? and How? Finish by describing the outcome of the war, and how it affected ancient Greece.

The ancient Greeks built powerful warships that gave them a huge advantage during wartime conflicts. The warship shown here, a *trireme* [TRY-reem], was the fastest vessel of the time, powered by the strength of 170 rowers. It had a wooden ram built below the waterline. The Greeks would crash this ram into the side of an enemy ship so it would sink.

Life in the City-States

The ancient Greeks believed that the state should be small enough that people would know their fellow citizens and be able to reach any place in the state within a day's walking.

The ancient Greeks called the household the *oikos*. It is the source of our word *ecology*. What connection do you see between the two words?

Reading Hint

As you read the next page, think about how life can differ depending on who you are, and what stage of life you're at.

The ancient Greek city-states were bustling places. Each was a thriving centre of the arts, religion, commerce, and politics. A strong, high wall encircled each city, keeping attackers and wild animals out. Inside the wall, built on top of a hill, was a fort, called an **acropolis** [uh-KROP-uh-lis]. The residents built their houses close together around the foot of the acropolis for protection.

The centre of the Greek city-state—and the place where everything was happening—was the **agora** [AG-uh-ruh]. This was the public square and marketplace combined. Surrounding it were temples, law courts, and public buildings.

The streets of ancient Greek cities were narrow and crowded. None of the cities had sewage systems, and garbage was thrown into the streets. Not everything about ancient Greece was what we think of as "civilized."

The people lived in simple homes. Even the wealthy lived in plain houses built of mud bricks with earthen floors. At the centre of each home was a courtyard with an altar where the family offered prayers to their many gods and goddesses. Men and women lived in separate parts of the house.

The people of the city-states worked at the many jobs the city provided, as craftspeople, builders, traders, farmers, and fishers. Slaves lived and worked in almost all households, doing most of the cleaning, shopping, cooking, and sewing. Under Greek law, owners could not mistreat their slaves. In some cases, slaves were allowed to buy their freedom if they received and saved a tiny wage.

Growing Up in Ancient Greece

If you had been born in ancient Greece, your life would have been very different depending on whether you were a girl or a boy, a slave or a citizen, wealthy or poor, young or old, married or widowed, an Athenian or a Spartan. (Sparta, as you'll see, was unlike any of the other city-states.)

Unless you lived in Sparta, here is what life would have been like for you if your parents were citizens of a city-state.

Age 0–6: Childhood

Your chances of growing up at all are better if your family is wealthy. If your father can't afford to feed you, he has the right to abandon you. If someone decides to take you in, you may be raised as a slave.

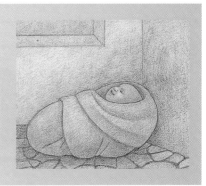

Age 6–14: School Days

If you're a girl, you do not go out to school. Your mother teaches you reading, writing, arithmetic, and the skills you'll need to run a household. If you're a boy, your school day lasts from sunrise to sunset. You learn reading, writing, poetry, arithmetic, drawing, and painting.

Age 14–16: Early Responsibilities

If you're a boy, your schooling ends, and your physical training begins. You spend the day working out at the public gym, playing sports, and running. If you're a girl, you marry the man your father chooses for you. Your father gives you a **dowry**—money, slaves, and cloth to take with you to your husband's home. Your husband is probably twice your age. Young men are expected to be soldiers for much of their early adulthood, so they aren't allowed to marry young.

Age 18–21: Reaching Adulthood

If you're a young woman, you are now a wife and mother. You spend your days at home, running the household. If you're a young man, you start your military service, which lasts for two years. You learn the art of war and good citizenship.

Adult Life

If you are a young man, you become a citizen at age 21. You live an active life, working, staying fit, and discussing politics. You attend festivals, the theatre, and sporting events. At age 30, you marry, but you spend little time with your wife and children. If you are a young woman, your life remains the same until your husband dies. You gain respect for the skill with which you raise your children, care for your husband, and manage your slaves.

A Closer Look

Sports as Part of Daily Life

If you are a sports-minded male, you would have felt right at home in ancient Greece. The ancient Greeks idolized physical health and strength, and young men were expected to keep themselves as fit as possible. Physical training was part of every young man's education. It was considered just as important as intellectual pursuits such as reading, writing, and mathematics.

The ancient Greeks valued sports, both as training for warfare and as a way of honoring the gods. They built gymnasiums for working out, and stadiums for competitions. Their athletic festivals attracted competitors from all over the ancient Greek world.

The most important athletic festival was the Olympic Games. All the Greek city-states took part in the games, which were held once every four years. The ancient Greeks even halted wars to allow their athletes to compete in the Olympic Games. People were expected to set aside their grudges and compete on the playing field instead of the battlefield. How are the modern Olympic Games similar?

Women could not take part in the Olympic Games, or even attend to watch. They had their own athletic contests. The most important of these were games held to honour the goddess Hera.

Historians decided that the **Classical Age** of ancient Greece—the period when ancient Greek civilization reached its height—began in 776 BCE. This was the year that ancient Greece held its first Olympic Games.

After a break of about 2000 years, the first modern Olympics were held in 1896 in Athens, where they were held in ancient times. Today the Olympics are held in a different place once every four years. Why would people have wanted to revive this ancient tradition?

Think For Yourself

Identify three reasons the ancient Greeks pursued physical fitness. Think of at least three reasons Canadians do so. How are the reasons alike and different?

Life in Sparta

Life was different in Sparta than in all the other city-states. In Sparta, loyalty to the state was of utmost importance. All Spartan citizens were expected to contribute to the military strength of the city. Toughness and discipline were the most admired characteristics in both men and women. From the age of 7 to the age of 20, all boys served as soldiers. Even as adults, men were expected to spend most of their time training and living with other soldiers.

In Spartan society, bearing children was highly respected as a great duty and accomplishment because it helped the state survive. Spartan women were also admired for raising their children to be strong and disciplined, and devoted to serving the state. Girls were expected to take part in athletic training so that they would have healthy children.

Women: Citizens with Few Rights

In ancient Greece, as in most ancient civilizations, women had few rights. People called this the will of the gods. They believed the gods expected men to rule over women, children, and slaves. Women were not allowed to participate in politics. They could not buy or sell anything.

Nor could they lend money or own property. They did not have a right to take someone to court.

A woman in ancient Greece had one major responsibility: running her household. She directed the work of the slaves, made the clothes, cooked the food, and raised her children. She gave her daughters as much education as she could. (Boys went out to school.)

A Greek woman could go out to attend the theatre and religious festivals, if her husband gave her permission, and if he agreed to accompany her. If a woman's husband died before her, his property went to his sons, though the woman kept her dowry. Her husband's will might name a new husband for her. If not, she returned to her father or another male relative.

The situation was quite different in Sparta than in the other ancient Greek city-states. Here, a woman could own property, represent herself in court, and take part in political decisions. Women probably had more freedoms in Sparta because the men were often away at war or in military training, so the women had to run things.

Spartans rejected all the comforts of life so they would be better prepared to defend their homeland. We still call a life that lacks comfort a Spartan existence.

Part of a Spartan mother's duty to the state was to punish her sons if they showed any signs of weakness or cowardice.

Some important Greek thinkers did not fully agree with the lack of rights for women. The famous Greek philosopher Plato wrote, "If women are to have the same duties as men, they must have the same education."

All ancient Greek women did household work. Nonetheless, they enjoyed a much better life than slaves, both male and female, who performed the hardest tasks.

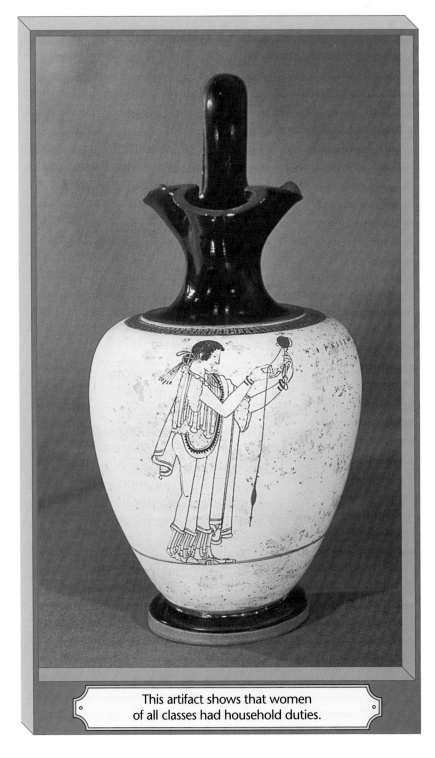

This artifact shows that women of all classes had household duties.

Try This

Draw a "power web" for ancient Greece. On a page, scatter the words *female citizen, female slave, male slave, male citizen,* and *children*. Then draw arrows showing who has power over whom. How would you describe the power structure?

Birthplace of Democracy

In most ancient civilizations, people had little say in their lives. Everyone followed rigid social rules. Rulers thought of ordinary people not as a collection of individuals, but as a group. This group was useful for building monuments, growing food, and paying taxes. As individuals, ordinary people just didn't count. Only the very powerful enjoyed true freedom.

From very early times, the ancient Greeks thought differently. They believed that all male Greek citizens—both rich and poor—had rights. Every Greek man enjoyed the same right to speak for himself, to be fairly treated, to take part in decisions, and to vote. Instead of being ruled by a monarch or a dictator, the ancient Greeks believed the people should choose rulers and vote on matters themselves. Here we have the beginnings of

democracy [dih-MOK-ruh-see]—rule by the people.

We don't know for sure why the ancient Greeks had such a different view of the individual. It may have been because ancient Greece was a collection of relatively small, self-governing city-states rather than a large country, like Egypt. At first, most power was in the hands of a few rich landowners. Over time, however, the rich came to rely more and more on soldiers and traders, who wanted more rights for themselves. Because the early city-states were small, every person would have had a role in ensuring the group's survival. Because every person was valued, the ancient Greeks may have seen the benefit of granting individual rights.

The Greek view that women should not have political rights endured for more than 2000 years. Even in Canada, women only received the right to vote in 1918.

The word *democracy* joins two Greek terms: *demos,* "people," and *kratos,* "rule"—in other words, "rule by the people."

Many people in the world still do not have the right to vote that the ancient Greeks first pioneered 2500 years ago. Sometimes democratic rights are not respected. For example, the people of East Timor [TEE-mor], such as the man in this photograph, were brutalized by gangs of thugs who disliked the outcome of a democratic vote about independence.

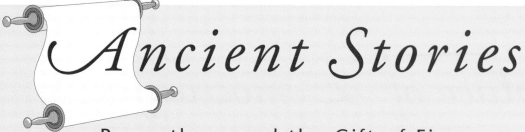

Ancient Stories

Prometheus and the Gift of Fire

Every culture has myths that help people understand how they came to be on earth, and how they came to acquire certain blessings. This ancient Greek myth shows both how humans were created, and how they acquired fire. Some myths also reveal the values of a society. As you read, think about the struggle of Prometheus [pruh-MEE-thee-us]. What does his battle with Zeus [ZOOS] tell us about what ancient Greeks valued?

The gloriously horrible Titans [TITE-unz] were borne of the gods Gaea [GAY-uh] and Uranus [yuh-RANE-us]. Prometheus, the wisest of the Titans, had always been loyal to the god Zeus, the supreme ruler of the universe. All that was to change.

One day, Zeus gave Prometheus the task of creating human beings out of mud. When Prometheus looked at his creations, he couldn't help but feel pity for them, for they seemed so small and helpless. Surely they would wither and die when they faced the great forces of nature. Prometheus decided to help them stay alive—he would give them fire. With fire, people would be able to keep wild animals away and cook their food.

But Prometheus did not own fire—the gods owned it. Nonetheless, Prometheus was determined to deliver his gift. He waited for many days until the gods were not looking. And then he stole a red-hot coal.

When Zeus found out what Prometheus had done, he went into a rage and tore at his hair. Prometheus would have to be punished! How could he be punished though? As a Titan, Prometheus was **immortal**—he would never die.

After many days, Zeus thought of a punishment that would be even worse than death. He sent his servants to chain Prometheus to a rock. "You dared to steal from me," he roared as his victim struggled in vain. "Now you will suffer for all eternity."

On Zeus's command, a terrible eagle flew down to the rock where Prometheus was chained. And as the great Titan pulled at his chains, the gigantic bird tore open his belly and yanked out his liver. That night, as Prometheus lay shivering in the cold, he was miraculously healed.

But the next day, the eagle returned and repeated his horrible task. And the next night Prometheus was again healed. And so it went.

Zeus offered to free Prometheus in exchange for a secret that only Prometheus knew. But Prometheus refused to tell his secret. Day after day, year after year, his will never weakened.

Hercules [HER-kyuh-leez], the half-human son of Zeus, saw how the brave Titan suffered, all because he had given fire to humans. He admired the Titan for refusing to give in to Zeus. One day, Hercules waited till the eagle landed on the rock. And then the strongest hero in the world caught the eagle and killed it. He smashed the chains that bound Prometheus; they broke apart as though they were made of straw.

Prometheus had succeeded in giving the valuable gift of fire to the mortals he pitied. He had endured long and terrible suffering because he had refused to give in to the will of Zeus. And now he was free. Yet in his heart, Prometheus had always been free.

Think For Yourself

Both Prometheus and Hercules are heroic characters in ancient Greek mythology. By looking at their characters and deeds, we can get an idea of the qualities admired by the ancient Greeks.

- Describe Prometheus's battle of wills with Zeus using the words "individual" and "supreme ruler."

- What does the story reveal about Greece's ideas concerning the individual?

Democracy in Athens

In most ancient Greek city-states, all free men and women were citizens. But out of 350 000 people living in Athens in the fifth century BCE, only 20 000 were male citizens. In Athens, women were considered to be citizens but without political rights.

Slaves and people from other city-states were not considered citizens, so they had no political rights. Slaves did enjoy some basic human rights. They could not be severely punished, and some could expect a small wage, which they could spend or save to buy their freedom. Former slaves would have been treated like people born outside the city-state—they were free to come and go, but had no other rights.

Athens was the largest and most powerful of the city-states. It was in Athens that the boldest form of government "by the people" appeared.

The Athenian democracy had two parts: the **Assembly** and the **Council**. All male citizens belonged to the Assembly, which made the laws of the land. They were expected to attend regular meetings to discuss and vote on public matters. If a meeting of the Assembly didn't have 6000 citizens present, police were sent out to round up more. The police used a rope dipped in red paint to shame the dawdlers.

The Council was made up of 500 citizens chosen every year by **lot**—names were drawn from all Athenian citizens. Members served for one year. The council did all the leg-work, preparing laws for the Assembly to consider.

Athenian citizens were also expected to serve as jurors in court cases. A typical jury had from two hundred to four hundred members. There were no judges or lawyers. Citizens argued their own cases.

Canadian society is too large for everyone to have a direct voice in all government decisions, so we elect representatives to speak for us (city councillors, for example).

The next time you get "roped in" to do something, you'll know where the phrase comes from.

The Assembly voted on laws and policies prepared by the Council.

The Assembly could exile unpopular or dishonest leaders. If at least 6000 citizens voted to remove a citizen from office, he would be sent out of the city for 10 years.

The Assembly elected government officials and military generals. This meant that even the poorest male citizen might find himself as a leader in the government.

All male citizens were expected to attend the meetings of the Assembly.

Red paint revealed who had to be dragged to the assembly to do their duty.

Think For Yourself

In Canada, we follow the democratic model of government first attempted by Athens 25 centuries ago. But there are many differences. Make a four-column table like the one begun below comparing the Canadian and Athenian systems of democracy. For each system, describe who qualifies as citizens, who can elect representatives, who can vote about laws, how many levels of government there are, how court cases are decided, and how unpopular leaders are dealt with. For each comparison, decide which system you think is better and why.

Points of comparison	Athenian system of democracy	Canadian system of democracy	Which works better? Why?
Who qualifies as citizens?	All free men and women. Not slaves.	All adults.	Canadian system works better because it's fair to all adults.

PERSPECTIVES

Democracy

Many Greek citizens feared that too much democracy could be a bad thing. Here is how one unhappy Athenian described his doubts about the new political freedoms in his land.

Everywhere the best people are opposed to democracy, because among the best element [the rich] there is least excess and injustice, and most self-discipline to useful ends. Among the [ordinary] people, on the other hand, ignorance is at its height, as well as disorder and vulgarity. For poverty, lack of education, and in some cases the ignorance which arises from lack of money lead them more to unseemly conduct...

... as it is, any scoundrel who pleases can get up, say his say, and get what is good for him and his like. It might well be asked, "What that is good for himself or for the state would such a man know?" But the people know that this man's ignorance, commonness, and good will profit them more than the virtue, wisdom, and disaffection of the conservative [the rich].

From John Trueman. *The Enduring Past: Revised Edition*, Toronto: McGraw-Hill Ryerson, 1967, p. 128

Try This

Giving speeches was an important part of life for citizens of ancient Greece. Put yourself back in time. Prepare a speech about democracy to give at the Assembly. Either agree with the view of democracy given in the Perspectives feature or oppose it.

HOW TO... Give a Persuasive Speech

A lot of people get nervous at the thought of speaking in front of others. It's only natural. Try to remember that the members of your audience are just like you—when it's their turn, they'll be nervous too.

You'll notice that people who are enthusiastic about a topic usually have no problems talking about it. How can you get enthusiastic? First, find a topic that really interests you. Second, get prepared. Comfortable speakers know their topic inside and out.

Here are some pointers for preparing a speech designed to persuade people to see your point of view.

1. Know exactly what you want to say. Sum up your position in one sentence.

2. Create a series of arguments to support your main idea. Ask yourself if each point you make supports your main idea.

3. Build support for your position by giving your listeners facts, examples, and details.

4. Find out about other points of view. In your speech, show how these arguments are wrong. If you don't, your listeners may think you're avoiding the tough questions.

5. Remember that the way you present your ideas is as important as the ideas themselves. Enthusiasm can be very convincing. Try not to act angry or sarcastic about the opposing point of view. Be honest, and your listeners will have more respect for your argument, even if they disagree.

6. Practise, practise, practise. Then, before you start speaking, take a deep breath and relax.

A Life of the Mind

Have you ever wondered about the meaning of life, how people should live together, why things turn out one way and not another? If you have, you are thinking about things that fascinated the ancient Greeks.

The ancient Greeks questioned everything in the universe. They valued knowledge and wisdom above everything else. Ancient Greek society honoured and glorified their philosophers just as much as they did their great athletes and warriors. They believed that it was a noble thing to seek wisdom because only through wisdom can one find the best ways to live.

So much of the Canadian way of life first appeared in ancient Greece that it is hard to name them all. Our democratic system of government, competitive sports, styles of architecture, ways of thinking and discussing, entertainment, literature, science, and mathematics—all these were influenced by the achievements of the ancient Greeks. Here are some of their most important discoveries.

Mathematics and Science

Most ancient cultures created myths to explain the things they did not understand. The ancient Greeks had myths, too, but they also attempted to find realistic explanations for the way things happened in the world and the universe. They believed that they could learn about the nature of things by using **reason**—they observed nature and asked questions. Reason became the basis of our method of scientific research.

The ancient Greeks made great discoveries in biology, mathematics, astronomy, and geography. They developed an advanced form of geometry, which they used to calculate the **circumference** [sur-KUM-frunce] of the Earth almost exactly. This means that they knew the Earth was round—knowledge that was lost for many centuries. The ancient Greeks were also far ahead of their time in suggesting that the Earth revolved around the Sun. At the time, most people believed that the Sun, moon, and stars all revolved around the Earth.

Medicine

The ancient Greeks were among the earliest people to make a distinction between medicine and both magic and religion. One of their most famous physicians was **Hippocrates** [hih-POK-ruh-teez]. He rejected the view that disease was sent as punishment from the gods. He believed that diseases had causes that could be treated. He and other ancient Greek physicians did not know much about diseases and their causes. In fact most of their speculations were plain wrong. It was their approach that was so influential.

The Hippocratic Oath. I swear ... that according to my ability, I will keep this oath: ... to follow that system of treatment which I believe will help my patients, and to refrain from anything that is harmful to them. I will give no deadly drug if I am asked to do so, nor will I recommend any such thing....

Hippocrates thought that all doctors should take this oath to guarantee that they would be honest and earnest in treating their patients. Doctors today still take the Hippocratic Oath when they graduate from medical school.

Arts and Architecture

All people had humble homes. Nonetheless, to be a citizen of ancient Greece was to live a life surrounded by great works of art. Instead of palaces for the rich, the ancient Greeks built magnificent theatres, temples, political buildings, and other public gathering places. Attending the theatre, temple, or agora was all part of a citizen's daily routine.

All ancient Greek public buildings were decorated with fine sculptures and murals. Sculpture was the finest of the Greek arts. The ancient Greeks admired the human form, and tried to capture it perfectly in their statues.

Ancient Greek and Roman architecture styles have long been known together as **classical architecture**.

The British Museum in London, England, was built to look like the Parthenon, the Acropolis of Athens. What similarities do you see in these two buildings?

The themes of ancient Greek stories and plays became the models for European writing. Shakespeare, for example, wrote tragedies, as did the ancient Greek playwrights.

Literature and Drama

The ancient Greeks built large theatres so that everyone in the city could attend. Plays were performed as part of religious festivals. People would spend the whole day at the theatre watching several plays—both comedies and tragedies. Like modern plays, they had directors, actors, costumes, and scenery. They also had a narrator in the form of a **chorus**— a group of people who commented on the action of the play by singing about it. Because ancient Greek plays tended to deal with universal issues, many are still performed and their plots copied.

Language

The ancient Greeks gave the world the first alphabet that had both consonants and vowels. It was this alphabet that developed into the Roman alphabet, which we use today to write English.

The Greek language spread throughout the Mediterranean as a language of trade. It was also the common language of the early Christians.

The ancient Greeks didn't just give us words; they gave us the ideas behind the words. From the words in this chart, what interests can you see that we share with the ancient Greeks?

Greek Word	Greek Pronunciation	English Equivalent
ΣΧΟΛΗ	schole	school
ΦΥΣΙΚΑ	physika	physics
ΓΑΛΑΞΙΑ	galaxia	galaxy
ΑΤΟΜΟΝ	atomon	atom
᾽ΑΡΜΟΝΙΑ	harmonia	harmony
ΣΤΑΔΙΟΝ	stadion	stadium

Try This

Make a Greek word tree. Start by writing a two-part word that comes to us from Greek, such as *autograph*, *biology, microphone,* or *hemisphere,* at the bottom of a page. Attach a new ending to the first part (*autocrat*) and a new beginning to the second part (*telegraph*). Now break each of your new words into two pieces and see if you can repeat the process (*automobile* and *democrat; telephone* and *pictograph*). See how big you can make your tree, making up your own new words if you run out of real words.

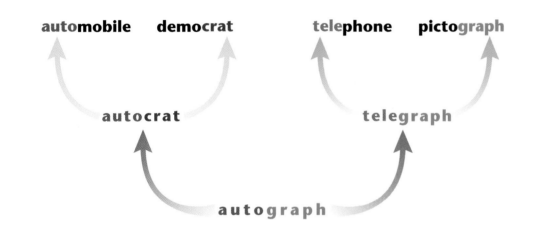

automobile   **democrat**   **telephone**   **pictograph**

autocrat   **telegraph**

autograph

Think For Yourself

Identify three ancient Greek innovations you read about in this section. Think about how they affect us today in everyday ways.

Looking Back

In this chapter, you have seen how the ancient Greeks lived and what they valued. Do you agree with the ancient Greeks that knowledge and wisdom are more valuable than anything else? How can knowledge and wisdom make life better for all people in society?

Chapter 9

Rome: Citizens and Slaves

W hen you think about life in Canada, do you see great promise or serious problems? Perhaps you see both.

When we look at the past, we see that life has always been full of **contradictions** [kon-truh-DIK-shuns]—things that seem to tell us two different stories at the same time. Wealth and poverty, laws and chaos, freedom and oppression—all these seem to occur at the same time in societies everywhere.

In this chapter, you can learn about the contradictions in the powerful Roman Empire. Historians often talk about the "grandeur of Rome" because of the great achievements of the energetic and practical Roman people. But ancient Rome was an empire built on slave labour and the conquest of nations. When you study this great civilization, you'll find the best and worst of what humans have accomplished. You might also find that the Roman civilization seems familiar. That's because our own civilization has so much in common—both good and bad—with Rome.

The Romans and Their Empire

Today you can find remains of Roman forts, roads, and bridges scattered across a vast region. You could visit the huge wall they built across northern England, a market in Turkey, or the ancient roads in Tunisia. The map on this page shows the many lands that were part of the Roman Empire between 100 and 200 CE. About 60 million people lived within this region—about one-fifth of the world's population at that time.

The Romans conquered much of the ancient world in Europe, northern Africa, and Asia, and then connected it all with a huge network of roads. These roads joined hundreds of cultures that had been isolated from one another. How did Roman roads "shrink" the world, just as the Internet is "shrinking" our world today?

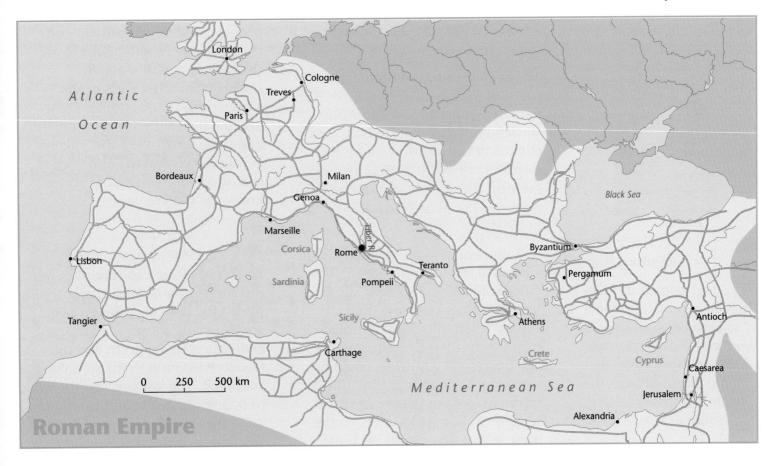

Atlantic Ocean

London
Cologne
Treves
Paris
Bordeaux
Milan
Genoa
Marseille
Corsica
Rome
Tiber R.
Teranto
Pompeii
Sardinia
Lisbon
Black Sea
Byzantium
Pergamum
Athens
Antioch
Tangier
Sicily
Crete
Cyprus
Caesarea
Carthage
Jerusalem
Mediterranean Sea
Alexandria

0   250   500 km

Roman Empire

How did the people of one ancient city come to be so powerful? The story is a long one, covering almost a thousand years. It begins in a group of villages occupied by a people known as the "Latins." Over hundreds of years, the Latins gradually conquered all the other peoples in their area. Taking advantage of the skills they had acquired as warriors, they then pushed beyond the lands they knew well. Eventually they controlled the greatest empire of the ancient world.

Try This

1. Work in a small group to compare the map of the Roman Empire with a current world map. Find and list the modern countries that were once part of the Roman Empire. Describe the extent of the empire.

2. Make a bar graph to compare the population of the Roman Empire in 150 CE (60 million) with the world population of the time (300 million). Describe the ratio.

3. Speculate on possible long-term effects of such a large portion of the world's population living under one rule.

In Roman times, Europeans knew few of the world's peoples, so it seemed that Rome ruled the world.

A Safe and Abundant Land

The early Latins lived on the plain south of the Tiber [TY-bur] River. The land here is flat and fertile, unlike the land in other parts of Italy. The climate of the region is warm, with plentiful rainfall. It is ideal for farming. The people found it easy to produce enough to feed a large population.

Rome began as one of many Latin villages along the Tiber River. This village offered an excellent site for a large settlement because it sat among seven hills. The hills made it hard for invaders to approach the city unseen. The hillsides could be seen from the city, and the hilltops served as lookout points. At the same time, Rome's location on the banks of the Tiber River meant that people could travel easily to and from the sea. People traded along the river and with sea-going traders from other parts of the Mediterranean. Over time, Rome became the centre for government and trade for all the Latin villages. It became so central to Latin society that the Latins eventually became known as the Romans.

An Ambitious People

Rome's location was important not just for its natural advantages. It also placed the Romans between two ancient civilizations: the Etruscan civilization to the north and the Greek civilization to the south and southeast. The Romans saw the value of taking the best ideas from these and other peoples and adapting them to their own use.

Reading Hint

Rome had many advantages that allowed it to become an empire. As you read this chapter, note Rome's natural advantages and the advantages the people themselves created, such as a huge army.

Try This

Three natural features made Rome ideal as a site for a city. These included the fertile, flat land nearby, the river that ran beside it, and the hills that surrounded it. In a three-column chart, make jot-notes describing how each feature made life easier for the Romans, and added to their growing power.

Fertile flat land	River location	Surrounding hills

Aqueducts are a type of bridge for supporting a water pipe over a river or valley.

The Etruscans were the wealthy trading people who had cleared the forests and begun farming in the area north of Rome. The Romans copied and developed their great engineering and artistic skills. In very early times, the Etruscans had ruled the Romans. They taught the Romans their techniques for making everything from wine and olive oil to ships and **aqueducts** [AK-wuh-dukts]. The Roman people despised their Etruscan rulers, however, for being cruel and greedy. They finally overthrew these rulers in 509 BCE.

The Romans also learned from the Greeks, who had many settlements south of Rome on the Italian Peninsula. The Romans used many Greek innovations, including Greek art and architecture, and even the Greek alphabet. They admired the Greeks' love of knowledge and excellence, and often brought Greeks to Rome to work as teachers. Most important, the Romans modelled their system of government and law on the democratic ideas of the Greeks.

The Romans learned many things from the Etruscans who ruled over them for so many centuries. For example, they learned how to make beautiful objects out of gold like the Etruscan jewellery shown here.

These artifacts show from whom Romans learned their gold-smithing skills.

From Village to Empire

Rome's story, from its beginnings as a collection of villages to its height as the centre of the European world, and then to the collapse of its great empire, took about 1000 years. During that time, the ancient Romans had three different forms of government: a monarchy, a democracy, and a dictatorship.

800–509 BCE
The Kingdom

Etruscan monarchs rule Rome. In a **monarchy**, kings or queens rule. The right to rule is inherited.

509 BCE–27 BCE
The Roman Republic

The Romans overthrow the Etruscans in 509 BCE. They set up a **republic**, which is a form of democratic government in which the people hold the power. Male citizens have the right to vote. The first laws are established.

27 CE–476 CE
The Roman Empire

In a series of wars, Roman generals fight for control of Rome. The republic is overthrown, and Rome becomes a dictatorship. In a **dictatorship**, one person—in this case, an emperor—holds all the power.

800 BCE	509 BCE	27 CE	476 CE

800   700   600   500   400   300   200   100   **0**   100   200   300   400

Important Events in the History of Rome

753 BCE	According to legend, twins named Romulus and Remus, who were brought up by a she-wolf, founded Rome.
450 BCE	Rome creates a code of laws called the Twelve Tables.
219 BCE	Hannibal crosses the Alps with elephants and attacks Rome.
146 BCE	Rome destroys Carthage.
49 BCE	Julius Caesar seizes control of Rome.
117 CE	The Roman Empire reaches its greatest extent.
410 CE	The Visigoths [VIZ-ih-goths], a Germanic people, sack Rome.
476 CE	Odoacer [oh-doh-AY-sur], a German, overthrows the last Roman emperor, Romulus Augustulus [ROM-yuh-lus uh-GUST-yuh-lus].

Try This

1. With a partner, research one of the events listed in the table above. Together, create an illustration of your event. Then, as a class, use your pictures to create an illustrated time line as a classroom display.

2. Take turns using your class time line to tell or dramatize the story of Rome.

Building an Empire

Strength of an Army

The Roman Empire expanded because its backbone—the army—was strong. By the time the Romans had conquered their neighbouring enemies, they had become expert warriors. Then, for almost 500 years, from around 300 BCE until 200 CE, Rome waged war. Rome's army first conquered all of Italy, and then defeated the Greeks. It spread west and east, capturing one land after another.

At first, the army was made up of Roman citizens. Most served for 20–25 years. Soldiers were trained not only to fight but also to build forts and roads. These were needed to control the **provinces**, as Rome's conquered lands were known. Many soldiers served as police officers, keeping the peace in the provinces. Even when assigned to work far from Rome, they built settlements with all the comforts of a Roman town.

While on the march, every Roman soldier carried a heavy load of tools, arms, and shield, as well as personal possessions. What advantages would this practice bring the army?

As the empire grew, the army hired soldiers from other lands.

Over their long history as warriors, the Romans became masters of warfare. Their army grew into the most organized and efficient in the ancient world. The strength of the Roman army came from tough discipline, effective weaponry, and skillful military strategy. Here are some examples of the advantages the Romans took into battle.

Armour: Roman soldiers wore curved plates of iron or steel to protect themselves from their enemies' swords.

Shields: The oblong, curved shields gave excellent protection. In battle, the Roman soldiers would use their shields to make a wall.

Troop Formation: The army was organized into **legions** of 4000 to 6000 soldiers. Each legion was made up of about ten units. Each of these was made up of six groups of 80 men and a commander. In battle, each group of 80 moved as a unit. The legion commander gave orders through trumpet signals.

Cavalry: The **cavalry**—soldiers on horseback—rode on both sides of the foot soldiers. Unlike soldiers in chariots, the cavalry soldiers could move quickly to any spot.

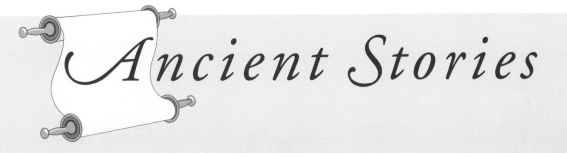

Ancient Stories

A Celtic Queen Battles the Roman Red Crests

The people conquered by the Romans often fought long and hard before they were defeated. The Celtic [KEL-tic] peoples who lived in what is now England were some of the most ferocious warriors the Romans encountered. Queen Boadicea [bode-ih-SEE-uh], or Boudicca [BODE-ih-kuh], as she is also called, was a Celtic queen. After the Romans seized her territory, she gathered a large army, destroyed the Roman settlements, and killed thousands of Romans.

This selection, from Song for a Dark Queen *by Rosemary Sutcliff, is a fictional account of the final defeat of the queen and her army by the Red Crests—the Roman army. The story is told through the eyes of the Queen's faithful record keeper. Here he describes the day when Queen Boadicea's Celtic army—the War Host—goes out to meet the Red Crests for the last time.*

The War Host rolled out from the forest … As many as though the leaves of the forest had fallen and turned into warriors. Men on foot and on horseback and in chariots, with their spears thirsty again after the long wait; and bringing up the rear, the great ox-wagons with the women and children … and the Queen with the chariot columns at the head of all. …

When word was brought to the Queen that the Red Crests [the Romans] were camped there for the night, no more than 10 000 … she laughed, and said, "Surely their gods have made them mad, that they have set themselves down in a trap, and we not having to lift a finger to drive them into it!" …

The Queen in her chariot … drove to and fro … reining in her dancing team to speak to the men…

"I would bid you see how few they are," she said. "But what are their numbers to us? We are a proud people fighting for our own. Think of the freedom they robbed us of, and that will be ours again, and … before the time comes to kindle this evening's cooking-fires, we shall have avenged old wrongs and be our own lords again!"

And everywhere the men laughed and shouted for her, "Boudicca! Boudicca!" and brought their spears crashing down across their shields in salute….

The Roman trumpets were yelping, and far off in the Red Crests' lines, the men who had been sitting or leaning on their spears, had straightened to become an unbroken wall of shield. And towards them our chariot line rolled forward … I felt the ground throbbing under my feet with the drum of hooves and the fury of chariot wheels as the great curved line swept on towards that waiting wall of Red Crests….

Nearer and nearer [the Celtic War Host] swept until they seemed almost upon the waiting Red Crests. And then in the last instant before the shock of meeting, [the War Host's] centre seemed to tear wide open like a horrible red wound.

[A flurry of spears had hailed down upon the War Host, stopping the best warriors in their tracks.] Horses were down … dragging their chariots with them; and the second wave of chariots, too close to pull clear, went crashing headlong into them, making a still more hideous confusion … suddenly the shape of the enemy was changing … it was becoming a wedge. A vast, terrible shield-flanked wedge, fanged and taloned with ripping sword-blades, driving into the gap that their spears had torn open for them, and thrusting on— and on.

The Red Crests' trumpets were screaming like angry hawks above the battle-roar; the shouted war cries and the shrieks of horses and the crash of splintering chariots.

The Queen … sprang into her chariot, and screamed something … was waving up the last reserves of chariots. I saw them hurtling forward like a winter skein of wild geese….

My throat was full of the smell of blood and sweat and the choking dust-cloud out of which men and horses reeled to and fro … Fresh waves of the enemy pressing in on us from the wings, cavalry bursting in upon our close-packed foot warriors, hacking their way through….

Our battle mass was being cut to rags—separate, desperate bands of men gathered about a chieftain … dying where they fell among the still-thrashing legs of wounded chariot ponies … Suddenly all around me men were running, with wide eyes and open mouths, some even flinging their spears away … And then I understood … It was not the Red Crests, but we, who were in the trap.

From Rosemary Sutcliff, *Song for a Dark Queen*, (London: Pelham Books Ltd. 1978), pp.150–57

Think For Yourself

Review the section on page 178 that describes some of the advantages the Roman army had over its opponents. Then reread the story above. As you read, jot down some notes under each of the following headings to explain how each influenced the outcome of the battle.

- The Roman spears
- The Celtic chariots
- The Roman cavalry
- The formation of the Roman foot soldiers

  Use your jot notes to discuss with a partner the Roman Red Crests' advantages over the Celtic War Host.

To make a list of jot-notes, write down important points, not necessarily in sentence form, nor in order of importance. Jot-notes help when you want to summarize something or write a paragraph.

Keeping an Empire

The Roman Empire bound millions of people together under a common official language and a common rule of law. People far from Rome ended up living, thinking, and speaking Latin like Romans. What language dominates in the world today?

Latin, the language of the Romans, became the main language of much of the empire. French, Spanish, and Italian all evolved from Latin. Even in English, almost half the words come from Latin.

*E*ach victory brought the Romans more strength and more land. But a bigger challenge for Rome was to keep its empire. Rome soon learned that it was better to embrace its former enemies than to destroy them. A destroyed city cannot become a trading partner.

Keeping Order

The Romans knew they could not rule their huge empire by force alone. Their victories usually ended with a **peace treaty**—an agreement

between two parties that want to stop fighting. Because Rome always won, the treaties always favoured Rome. For example, taxes were paid to Rome, not the other way around. Despite this, Rome ruled its conquered peoples in a way that made them feel part of the empire.

By providing the people they defeated with some of the benefits of being Roman, Rome could keep the peace. People were allowed to travel and trade anywhere within the empire. Roman laws protected their rights. Eventually, Roman citizenship was given to everyone in the empire except slaves. In return for loyalty to Rome, conquered people were allowed to keep their customs and, to a certain extent, govern themselves.

The Roman government also brought services to the people in their provinces. It provided soldiers to work as builders, engineers, and farmers. They built towns and cities connected by excellent roads. Roman soldiers drained marshes and cleared forests to make fertile farmland.

As long as the people of the empire worshipped Roman gods and goddesses, they were permitted to worship their own gods as well. Roman deities eventually included several dead emperors, such as Augustus, whose statue is shown here.

Although many conquered peoples were forced to work on these massive projects, the projects themselves were usually beneficial to all.

The Romans took Greek ideas of government and used them to shape a system of government based on laws and rules. They developed laws for almost everything—inheritance, women's rights, money dealings, treatment of slaves, and the behaviour expected of citizens. Over time, all people under Roman rule could depend on the same laws.

People in Rome's provinces were not all happy with Roman rule. After all, their way of life was changed—usually forever—after it fell under Roman rule. Languages disappeared, lands were seized and given to wealthy Romans, and people found themselves with a new government that they had not chosen. Some people merely lost their freedom to rule themselves; others lost all their freedom because the Romans made them slaves.

Travellers today find that certain products, films, and fashions appear wherever they go. Most of these are American, like the soft drink advertised on this wall in India. What similarity do you see between modern and Roman times?

Try This

1. As a group, discuss the pros and cons that faced communities that were ruled by the Romans. Record your ideas on chart paper, using a T-chart with pros on one side and cons on the other.

2. Think about the following statement and question and jot down some of your thoughts.

   "The Roman government used its power to improve the lives of its citizens. How was its use of power similar to and different from the way other ancient governments used their power?"

   Read the example in the chart at right, and think of two other examples.

Similar goal	Different use of power
Both the Greeks and Romans increased their citizens' wealth by creating trade.	The Romans got new trading partners by conquering other lands, whereas the Greeks increased trade by starting colonies.

A Closer Look

Public Works

The Romans were some of the greatest builders and engineers of the ancient world. With the wealth that flowed into Rome—from trade, taxes, and conquests—it paid for huge public-works projects throughout its empire. The Roman army built bridges and roads, forts and meeting halls, aqueducts and public baths.

The Romans built many structures from concrete. They were the first people to combine sand, stone, cement (lime and clay), and water to make concrete. These ingredients were cheaper and easier to transport than stone and made long-lasting structures.

Though they had no bulldozers, dynamite, or power tools, the Romans connected their empire with thousands of kilometres of bridges and roads. This road in Italy is called the Via Appia. Many like it are still in use today. Do you think the road in front of your school will last for 2000 years?

Water was brought into Roman towns and cities through aqueducts like this one in Spain (at right). This one was built of stones, with no mortar (cement). It still carries water today.

Romans built many public baths like this one in England. Every day, they would go to the bath, get their skin oiled and scraped by their servants, and then relax in a series of hot and cold pools. It was a great place to chat with friends.

Economic Opportunities for All

Rome gained enormous economic power through its position as the largest centre of trade in the ancient world. Goods poured into the city from the lands of the empire and beyond. With each new province, Rome gained another trading partner. The new province also gained trading partners, so everyone enjoyed a better standard of living.

The Roman army and laws eventually brought peace to many countries. Around 100 CE, Emperor Hadrian halted the conquest of new lands. He concentrated instead on keeping peace and order throughout the empire. This period of peace lasted about 200 years. The Roman soldiers made it safe to travel long distances over good roads. Roman towns became centres where people travelled to buy and sell goods.

Ever heard the saying, "All roads lead to Rome"? Now you know why they do.

Rome was rich in everything the world had to offer because Rome's superb network of roads allowed traders from all over to travel easily. Rome's army and laws kept the peace, so traders felt safe when they travelled to lands they didn't know well.

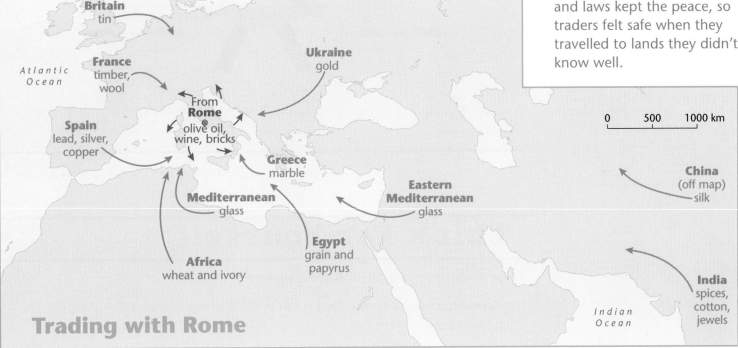

Trading with Rome

Try This

The Romans maintained a vast empire for over a thousand years. Running an empire, however, is a task riddled with problems. Make a web with "Running an Empire" at the centre. List various problems in bubbles at the next level, and Roman solutions at the third level. Copy the one below, and enlarge it.

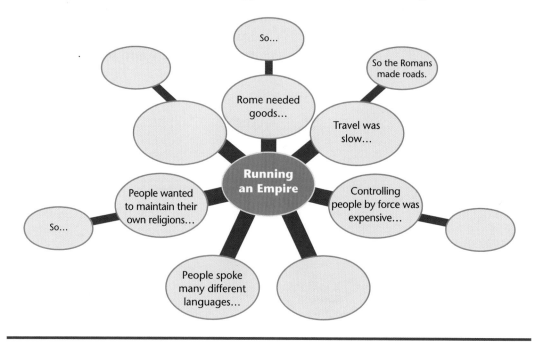

Think For Yourself

Agree or disagree with the following statement.

"**Communications technology** (*tools people use to communicate*) *always improves peoples' lives.*"

Give reasons for your opinion, using an example from Roman times and an example from modern times. Meet with another person to share your thinking.

Life in Rome

The wealth of the empire made the city of Rome the greatest tourist attraction of the ancient world. At least for the wealthy, the city was a place full of entertainment and luxuries. It was exciting for everyone. The city boasted glorious temples, bustling open-air markets, **amphitheatres**, huge theatres called forums, and public baths where you could relax after a busy day.

Wealthy Romans enjoyed extreme luxury. Most of their homes had servants' quarters, a small bathroom with a toilet that piped water into the sewers, and a walled garden. Some even had an early form of central heating that heated the floors.

Rome was also home to the many slaves and workers who made the luxuries of the wealthy possible. By 100 CE, slaves made up 400 000 of the million inhabitants of the city. The typical apartment blocks of working-class people were crowded and unsafe. Homes usually had one or two rooms. They had no running water; people shared public bathrooms instead. Fires often broke out from cooking fires and candles.

An amphitheatre [AM-fih-thee-uh-tur] is a round building with raised seats surrounding a central open space.

The homes of the wealthy were spacious and elaborately decorated. Tiles were laid out in intricate patterns to create beautiful mosaics on the floors and walls. Furniture was designed for comfort.

A Closer Look

The Attractions of the City

Imagine going back in time to visit Rome at the height of the empire. As you wandered through this crowded city, your eyes would feast on the wonders and shrink at the horrors. Here are some of the sights you wouldn't want to miss.

1 Colosseum [kal-uh-SEE-um]: Spend an afternoon watching professional fighters called gladiators fight each other—or perhaps a lion or tiger—to the death. Seating 50 000 people, the Colosseum is the largest amphitheatre in the Roman world.

2 Circus Maximus: The Circus Maximus is just one of five chariot-racing stadiums. Join 250 000 Romans at a time to watch races and athletic contests. When the circus is flooded, you can even watch sea battles.

3 The Baths of Trajan [TRAY-jun]: Rome has more than 170 public baths. They're a great place to unwind. Take your pick of marble gymnasiums for ball playing and wrestling, gardens for walking, libraries, steam rooms, and hot and cold pools.

4 The Forum : Visit the large, open-air market and the many shops, temples, and government buildings that surround it. While you're here, see the nearby tomb of Romulus, founder of Rome.

5 The Aqueduct of Claudius: You can't help but run into this structure. It travels right through the city, carrying water to the baths and to people's homes.

6 Temple of Venus and Roma: You'll find beautiful statues here, as well as in the Temple of Jupiter and the Temple of Caesar, nearby.

Try This

Choose one of Rome's many attractions shown or described in the Closer Look feature on the previous pages. Find out a little more about it, and what it looks like. How does it contribute to the excitement of Rome? Make a poster about this attraction to convince families to make the journey to this bustling city.

The Roman Social Structure

From early times, the Romans divided their society into two classes: citizens and non-citizens. If you were a free man born in Rome, you were a citizen with the right to vote and to be elected to government. Roman law protected you. Rome needed soldiers to run its empire, however, so you had to serve in the army. If you were sent to command a wealthy province, you could send a fortune back to your home in Rome from profits you made as a landowner or trader. If you were a free woman born in Rome, you were also considered a citizen but you could not vote. You could inherit property and ask for a divorce.

Non-citizens were either slaves or people born in the provinces. Non-citizens had few rights, and could not vote or hold political office. In 212 CE, all free men in the empire became Roman citizens.

Rome further divided all male citizens into two classes:

The Romans used slaves to do the work, but then had to provide free food to unemployed citizens, who were left with no way to make a living. The wealthy must have known that their comforts would end if they didn't at least feed the poor.

patricians [puh-TRISH-uns] and **plebeians** [plih-BEE-unz]. Patricians were the wealthy, privileged class of landowners. *Patrician* comes from *patres*, which means "fathers." The patricians were supposed to be descended from Rome's early tribal chiefs.

The working people were called "plebeians." Even though plebeians enjoyed the rights of citizenship, they had little wealth. They were valued because they served as soldiers. To keep the empire together, the patricians gradually gave more and more rights to the plebeians.

Like the Greeks, the Romans searched for ways to make life better for everyone. They made tremendous advances in their society. They developed laws, expanded trade, and built great public buildings. But like the Greeks, they did not consider all people to be equal members of their society. If you were a citizen or a slave, a patrician or a plebeian, a man or a woman, everything in life depended on which side of the divide you were on.

A Closer Look

Slavery

Even as the Romans worked to improve the rights of citizens, they depended more and more on slave labour. Many ancient civilizations relied on slave labour, but none as much as Rome. Slaves built the great temples and palaces, farmed the huge country estates of the rich, served in households, and worked as craftspeople. A wealthy patrician might own 500 slaves; an emperor would own thousands.

Slaves were often enemy soldiers captured during warfare. They were sold at public auction in Rome, with their country of origin marked on a sign around their neck. In the early days of Rome, poor people could be sold into slavery to cover a debt.

Eventually, slaves did benefit from Rome's tradition of rule by law. For example, for many years owners could force their slaves to work as **gladiators**—men who fought each other or wild animals for public entertainment. Laws were written to outlaw this practice. Laws were also passed forbidding slave owners from killing or abandoning slaves who became too old or sick to work.

The contrast between Rome's moral strengths and weaknesses has fascinated historians for centuries. Were the Romans cruel masters or wise leaders?

Think For Yourself

Imagine you are the Roman emperor. Create a plan to reform the social structure so that the well-being of the city will be preserved. Decide which class divisions you will have, and the rights and responsibilities of each group. Make a list of the changes you would make to achieve your goal.

The End of an Empire

For several centuries, Rome brought peace, law, and order to most of the provinces of the empire. Then gradually the empire began to erode. As Rome grew weaker within, invading tribes from beyond the Roman frontiers attacked. Finally, even the city of Rome fell to invaders.

The Romans thought their world would last forever. Why did it fall? For centuries people have tried to understand what caused the powerful Roman Empire to decline. Here are some of the factors that many historians believe led to Rome's fall.

- The fate of Rome was threatened when **it abandoned the Greek ideal of democracy** and became a dictatorship. Dictators cannot be voted out of office, so they don't have a good reason for trying to be good leaders.

- The **army hired soldiers from distant provinces**. These included the Visigoths, a Germanic people who had little loyalty to Rome. As they became more responsible for running things outside Rome, Rome lost control over its provinces.

- Ambitious **army generals fought for control** of the empire and used the army to help them gain power. But when soldiers supported a general, they always expected favours from the leader they had chosen. If they didn't get what they wanted, they murdered him. In a period of 70 years near the end of the empire, 23 emperors came to power; 22 of them were murdered.

- The Roman army was huge, but not large enough to defend the empire's **many long borders**.

- As Rome's wars with hostile peoples went on, **trade was disrupted**. After the flow of goods into Rome slowed down, so did the economy of the city and the entire empire.

As the cities of the Roman Empire fell, everything the Romans knew disappeared. The arts show this most clearly. In the ancient Roman sculpture shown at left, the horse seems almost lifelike. Compare this with the painting, at right, made many centuries later.

- The **gap between rich and poor** in Rome led to constant social unrest. To control the poor, Rome needed huge armies. To pay for the armies, Rome raised taxes even higher, which led to further social unrest.

- **Rome's dependence on slaves** weakened the Roman economy. Because slaves did most of the work, the common people had no jobs, so they couldn't contribute to the economy.

- The **spread of Christianity** challenged the Roman rule of state law. The Christian religion, which began in what was then the Roman province of Israel, was popular with slaves, the poor, and women. Unlike other religions, it offered every person the same promise of eternal life in heaven after death. The Christians refused to worship Roman deities.

The emperors provided "bread and circuses"— free food, chariot racing, and gladiator fights—to keep people from rioting. But it was not enough.

Try This

Make a cause-effect chart. Under "Cause" list the possible causes for the fall of the Roman Empire. You'll find these highlighted above and on page 192. For each cause, describe its effect—how it might have contributed to the decline of Roman civilization.

Cause	Effect
Rome abandoned democracy.	Rome was ruled by dictators. Many of them were bad leaders.

Looking Back

In this chapter, you have learned about a mighty empire that accomplished great things for its people and left a valuable legacy for the peoples of the future. We inherited much of what was bad about the Roman Empire, as well as what was wonderful about it. How much of Rome—both good and bad—do you see in our civilization today?

Chapter 10

World Connections

You've been reading the newspaper or watching the news on television for several years now. What's your impression? Do you think that thousands of years of civilization have made the world a better place to live?

That's a hard question to answer. In some ways, our world seems as violent and uncaring as it ever was. In the news, for example, we learn about wars, crimes of injustice, murders, theft, fighting, and many other conflicts.

In other ways, our world seems better than ever before. Over the last few decades, people around the world have become far more sensitive to issues of human rights. In the news, we read and hear about people trying to improve life for everyone on the planet. These people are active citizens.

As you read this chapter, ask yourself what kind of world you want to live in and what you can do to make the world a better place.

Citizenship and You

If you had to give evidence of your **citizenship** [SIT-uh-zun-ship]—what would you provide? You probably have legal documents such as a birth certificate, certification of citizenship, or a passport. Adults might also have a driver's licence and a SIN card. To many people, however, citizenship means much more than just pieces of paper.

What does citizenship mean to you?

We asked this question of students in Ms. Sneddon's Grade 7 class at Royal Oak Middle School in Victoria, BC. On the next two pages, you can read what some of the students said.

Citizenship comes from "civitas," the Latin word for "city." In general terms, *citizenship* means membership in a society.

What documents do you have that prove your citizenship or legal status in Canada?

Citizenship gives you protection and security in your own country. You should be unconditionally accepted in your country. This is not the case in some countries. You may not be accepted because of your religion or beliefs. I am proud to be a Canadian citizen and have a voice and stand up for what I believe in. Hopefully we will be treated with the same respect forever.

Warren Pratt

Imagine yourself in a busy and beautiful city. You walk along the street minding your own business. People stare and whisper, laughing and pointing. People yell at you, call you names, ... say you're out of place. People throw rocks and push you into the street. That is what it's like for some people!

Citizenship is very important in life. Really, it's just a word, but it means a lot. It means to be respected by people who are alike and people who are different. It means to be accepted by others without any argument. If you are a citizen you should feel safe and comfortable whatever your religion or beliefs. To be a citizen is like hanging out with (the) coolest people at your school. Most of us take it for granted.

Chelsea Burns

Students worked in small groups to express their views about what citizenship meant to them. This group put the results of their brainstorm on a web. What words would you include on a web about citizenship?

me being a citizen doesn't mean just getting, it also means giving to your community. Being a citizen entitles you to the rights and laws that protect you and your city. You also have to give to your community. You can volunteer at organizations like the S.P.C.A., like I do, or volunteer at an organization to help those with cancer. Another thing you can do is donate. Donations of food or money help make a good citizen too. To be a citizen you have to accept laws and help anyone who needs help. I also think keeping informed about events in your community is important. I think being a good citizen is being a good human being.

Lynne Bezuidenhout

One may think being a Canadian citizen isn't such a big deal, but it's pretty disturbing to hear about people getting driven out of their homes and fleeing their country just to stay alive. Your country is your home, so take good care of it. Respect the differences of its people and the beauty of our surroundings. We are lucky to live here, so be a good citizen!!!

Harrison Parker

Think For Yourself

Write three words or phrases that best describe what Canadian citizenship means to you. Meet with a partner and compare your words and phrases.

Driven From Home

Sometimes it's easier to figure out what something means to you when it's taken away. Think what it might be like if invaders forced you to leave Canada. They take all your belongings except what you can carry. They take away all your papers of citizenship, including your passport, birth certificate or certificate of citizenship, and even your library card. Who are you? Do you have any rights or freedoms any more?

Perhaps you think this could never happen to you. But it has

happened many times in history, and it's still happening.

On March 24, 1999, Serbian troops began forcing hundreds of thousands of ethnic Albanians to leave their homes in Kosovo [KOS-uh-vuh]. The soldiers killed many Albanians. Many more died on the terrible journey to the neighbouring republics of Macedonia [mas-uh-DOH-nee-uh], Albania [al-BANE-ee-uh], and Montenegro [mon-tuh-NAY-groh].

Since the end of World War Two, Kosovo has been a province of Serbia, the main republic in the

This relief, dated 695 BCE, shows an Assyrian soldier escorting Jewish musicians into exile. Think of another refugee event from ancient history.

This artifact shows that refugees existed in ancient times.

Uncertain of their future, these ethnic Albanians from Kosovo wait for a solution in a refugee camp in Macedonia in 1999. Think of another refugee event from modern times.

John Nadler, journalist in the Balkans

former Yugoslav federation. After Yugoslavia broke up, Serbian soldiers drove the Albanians away because they said Kosovo was theirs—the birthplace of the Serbian Orthodox Church and the location of the first Serbian kingdom in the Middle Ages. Yet the Albanians have been living in Kosovo for at least 300 years.

John Nadler, a journalist working in the Balkans, interviewed Besim Zeqiri, a young man driven from his home in Kosovo. When Zeqiri told his story, people were still being killed in Kosovo. Nadler wrote the article on the next page from his interview notes. In it, you can learn about how one young man felt when his citizenship was taken away from him.

"... I'VE BEEN ERASED"

By John Nadler

SKOPJE, MACEDONIA — Only days after being driven from the Yugoslav province of Kosovo, Besim Zeqiri, 27, a young journalist, sat in a cafe in Skopje, Macedonia and confessed his fear that he would never be able to return to his homeland again.

"I'm afraid that they will win," said Besim, speaking of the Serb police [officers] who forced him at gunpoint to leave the place where his ancestors have lived for thousands of years. "I'm afraid that I will leave Macedonia and find a job and a life in another country and forget about Kosovo. I'm afraid that I'll forget I'm a Kosovar, and that Kosovo will no longer exist.

"I feel like I've been erased."

For Zeqiri and thousands of other ethnic-Albanian refugees, to live life

When Yugoslavia broke up, ancient grudges resurfaced.

outside of Kosovo is to exist without an identity. To be a non-person. Kosovo is a province in the heart of the Balkans, a region in southern Europe, which has been the scene of some of the world's worst wars. Over the past 2000 years, Kosovo has been conquered by the Romans, Byzantine Greeks, Slavs, Ottoman Turks, Hapsburg Austrians, and Serbs. As descendants of the ancient Illyrians [a people that lived in the western Balkans], the Albanians, who once made up 90 per cent of Kosovo's population of two million citizens, say they are the oldest people in the Balkans. And they say they have paid dearly for their right to live in Kosovo. Their people have lived under many cruel regimes, and they love their home because so many of their forefathers died to be Kosovar.

"This is not your country," Serb soldiers reportedly told Kosovar Albanians. "Your country is Albania." Serbians claim Kosovo as their own because it once belonged to them.

But for many Albanians, Kosovo is their country because they live there now. "Kosovo is ours," said Zeqiri. "It is where we were born. I'll never be a complete person until I go back. And I will go back. Someday. No, I won't let myself be erased."

Try This

Answer these questions to help you think about what citizenship means.

- Why did the Serb soldiers believe Besim Zeqiri had no right to be a citizen of Kosovo?

- Why did Zeqiri think he had a right to be a citizen of Kosovo?

- What do you think Zeqiri meant when he said he felt like he had been "erased"?

- Make a list of all the things you would lose if you lost your citizenship like Zequiri did. How would this make you feel?

Citizenship

Active citizens believe that we need to balance our rights with our responsibilities.

When Women Got the Vote

Canada:	1918
United States:	1920
Great Britain:	1928
Switzerland:	1971

Over the year, you have looked at how the rights and responsibilities of individuals differed within several ancient civilizations, including Mesopotamia, Egypt, India, China, Greece, and Rome. Each civilization had a social structure that defined what people could and could not do. Over time, social structures began to change. Ordinary people became more involved in making decisions that affected their society. As they became more involved, people claimed the rights and responsibilities of citizenship.

Citizenship Through Time

In many ancient civilizations, one ruler made all the decisions about the society. Rulers decided who would have property and who would be a slave—and in some cases who would live and who would die. The ruler decided when to plant in spring, whether to go to war or keep the peace, and whether or not to feed the poor in times of drought. In some civilizations, like Egypt, the ruler chose trusted people to take charge of particular projects, but the ruler usually had the final say. Civilizations like Egypt had classes of people such as royalty, scribes, craftspeople, peasants or common people, and slaves. Most societies gave different status to men and women. Most ancient civilizations did not regard ordinary people as citizens with a right to help run society.

Greece

Citizenship, as we think of it, began in Greece. Not everyone in Aristotle's city-state of Athens was a citizen. In ancient Greece, only the free men in

In many nations, women still do not have equal rights. If not for protestors like those shown here, Canadian women might still lack political rights.

the cities were thought of as citizens. This classification left out slaves, women, foreigners, and people without property.

Aristotle, an ancient Greek philosopher, once said, "A citizen is not a citizen because he lives in a certain place." Instead, he said, a citizen is one who "shares in the administration of justice, and in [public] offices." Ancient Greek citizens helped run their society by electing people to office, and by holding office themselves.

Rome

The ancient Romans also kept citizenship from slaves, foreigners, and anyone without property. Women were considered citizens, but with no political rights. Both the upper classes (patricians) and the lower classes (plebeians) could vote and hold office. The patricians had more power, however, and in the early days of the Republic did not have to obey the laws made by the plebeians. In the days of the Roman Empire, the idea of equal citizenship came to include nearly every man who was not a slave.

Britain

When Rome fell, democracy disappeared from Europe. For about 1500 years, monarchs held all the power. By the nineteenth century, the situation had changed in many countries, including Britain. Wealthy landowners held the power and all male citizens with property could vote. Most men did not own property, however, so they could not vote. The wealthy landowners were concerned that letting all men vote would weaken the landowners' power to make laws that suited them.

In 1867, a new act of government gave the vote to men who were skilled city workers. In 1884, another act gave it to all men. Women were granted the vote in 1928.

United States

The Constitution of the United States of 1787 prevented all African Americans from having either **civil rights** or **human rights**. Between 1800 and 1830, most states passed laws allowing Caucasian men to vote. Caucasian women received the vote much later, in 1920. In 1965, new laws guaranteed that African Americans had the right to vote. Before this time, many African Americans were prevented from voting because some states used threats and laws to prevent them from doing so. Still today, in some parts of the world, many people of colour are denied the same rights and freedoms as Caucasian citizens.

Canada

In Canada, the idea of citizenship developed gradually. Early in its history, a Canadian was a citizen of the British Commonwealth. This consists of former members of the British Empire. Today, Canadians are citizens of Canada. Our head of state is Queen Elizabeth the Second, but all the political power rests in the politicians. Canadian citizens elect representatives to serve as members of Parliament. As Canadians, we enjoy many rights and freedoms.

Civil rights ensure that all citizens have equal protection under law and equal opportunity to exercise the privileges of citizenship regardless of race, religion, or sex. Human rights are the basic rights to which all humans are entitled. This includes the right to freedom.

Canada continues to recognize the status of Commonwealth citizenship, so Canadians can travel to any country in the Commonwealth without a **visa**. A visa is a stamp on a passport. It gives a person permission to enter a foreign country.

Today we define a legal citizen as an individual who is entitled to the rights and freedoms of a country because he or she was born there or went through the legal process of becoming a citizen.

Qualifications for Canadian Citizenship

What qualifies a person to be a Canadian citizen?

- By law, all persons born in Canada are Canadian citizens.

- Children born outside Canada are Canadian citizens if at least one parent is Canadian.

- People from other countries can become **naturalized citizens** (people of foreign birth who become Canadians). They can do so after they reach 18 years of age. They must come to Canada legally, and gain landed immigrant status. They must live in Canada for three years. In that time, they have to learn about Canada and the responsibilities of citizenship. They must also show some ability to speak either English or French.

The Oath of Citizenship

From this day forward, I pledge my loyalty and allegiance to Canada and Her Majesty Elizabeth the Second, Queen of Canada. I promise to respect our country's rights and freedoms, to uphold our democratic values, to faithfully observe our laws and fulfil my duties and obligations as a Canadian citizen.

In late 1999, the Government of Canada proposed this new Oath of Citizenship. New Canadians make this oath when they become citizens. What four things must they promise to do?

After fulfilling all the requirements, potential Canadian citizens become Canadians when they take the Oath of Citizenship.

Rights and Freedoms in Canada

Around the world, the citizens of Canada are known as a friendly people who respect differences. People from many countries think of Canadians as a people committed to the pursuit of human rights for all. This was not always the case. Canadian history includes times when people in Canada were intolerant, **prejudiced**, and **discriminated against** others, both foreigners and other Canadian citizens. Instances of these occur even today.

- For many years, starting in 1885, the Canadian government required all Chinese immigrants to pay a **head tax** (a certain amount per person) before entering the country. No other immigrants had to pay this tax.

- Vancouver's city papers of 1886 prevented all Chinese, Hindus, and Japanese from voting in local elections. They did not get the right to vote until 1947.

- In 1914, 376 British subjects (12 Hindus, 24 Muslims, and 340 Sikhs) of Indian origin arrived in Vancouver harbour aboard the *Komagata Maru*. As citizens of the British Commonwealth, they had the right to enter Canada. Nonetheless, Canada forced 352 of the passengers to leave.

Without knowing the whole story, some people protested when three ships of people fleeing China landed on the shores of British Columbia in 1999.

- During World War One, the Canadian government put about 5000 Ukrainian immigrants into camps and forced them to work in parks, logging, and steel mills.

- Canadian women were not considered "persons" under the law until 1929. Only after a widely circulated petition was presented to government, was the situation clarified in the Constitution Act, 1982, which includes the Charter of Rights and Freedoms.

- During World War Two, Canada seized the property of Japanese-Canadians and put them into prison camps.

- Before 1949, Aboriginal Canadians did not have the right to vote.

A prejudiced person is one who dislikes or distrusts a person or group because of wrong assumptions. To discriminate against a person or group is to act on those opinions.

Students in Ms. Sneddon's Grade 7 class explore the ideas of discrimination, prejudice, and intolerance in many different ways. This picture shows a **tableau** [TAB-loh] they created to show their understanding of discrimination. In a tableau, the performers all freeze in a position at the same time. The "picture" they make tells a story. What story does this tableau tell you?

Try This

In a small group, develop a tableau or collage to show your understanding of one of these ideas: prejudice, tolerance, equality, discrimination, or unity. Begin by finding a definition of your chosen concept in a dictionary. Discuss how you might use body positions or symbols to demonstrate the idea. Then work co-operatively to develop your presentation.

Citizenship can guarantee our membership in Canadian society. But the examples of intolerance in Canadian history show us that citizenship by itself cannot guarantee our rights and freedoms. What could give us such a guarantee?

Canada chose to write a document and make it the fundamental law of our land. It's called the Canadian Charter of Rights and Freedoms. The Canadian government and all Canadians must obey the rules in the Charter. These rules guarantee the rights and freedoms of all Canadians equally.

A Closer Look

The Charter of Rights and Freedoms

The Charter of Rights and Freedoms guarantees certain rights and freedoms to all Canadian citizens. These rights and freedoms include democratic, legal, equality, and language rights. As you read the following list, identify any rights or freedoms that you didn't know you had. If you're not a Canadian citizen yet, identify what rights and freedoms will be new to you.

Democratic Rights

• Canadians have the right to freedom of conscience, religion, thought, belief, opinion, expression, and peaceful assembly.

• Canadians have the right to enter, remain in, and leave Canada.

Legal Rights

• Canadians cannot be searched, detained, or imprisoned without reason.

• On arrest or detention, Canadians must be told why right away.

• Canadians charged with a crime have a right to a fair, reasonably prompt, public trial.

• Canadians must not be treated cruelly or given unusual punishments.

Equality Rights

• Canadians have the right not to be discriminated against because of race, national or ethnic origin, colour, religion, sex, age, or mental or physical disability.

Official Languages of Canada

• Canadians have the right to use the English or French language in all their dealings with the government of Canada.

Minority Language Educational Rights

• In certain circumstances, Canadians have the right to be educated in either official language, English or French.

Here is an example of Canadians exercising a right under the Canadian Charter of Rights and Freedoms. Which right or freedom applies?

Try This

1. Consider the situations listed below. Identify which of the Canadian Rights and Freedoms applies in each case.

    - A Canadian family decides to take a trip to Europe. They know they can exit and enter Canada freely.

    - A physically disabled person takes a restaurant owner to court because he refused to serve her.

    - A family moves into a new community. The parents ask the local school board to educate their children in French.

    - A Canadian court excuses a citizen charged with theft after she has waited more than a year for her trial date.

2. What does it mean to you to be a Canadian citizen? Create a collage including important ideas and symbols that represent being Canadian. Include images related to each of the following aspects of Canada:

    - culture and society

    - politics and law

    - economy and technology

    - environment

Think For Yourself

Agree or disagree with the following statement.

"The world is a better place to live today than it was in ancient times."

Support your opinion by comparing the lives of people from an ancient civilization with the lives of people today. Meet with another student to share your thinking.

Making the World a Better Place

When you value something, do you try to protect it? Throughout history, people have valued their citizenship in society. Because they felt a sense of responsibility towards their society, many did their best to protect it. Some people fought wars to protect their homelands. Some built public buildings to improve life for all. Some struggled to improve people's rights. These are active citizens—the people who make a difference.

Throughout history, there have always been people who made a difference because they cared deeply about a cause. The same is true today. Some of them are famous people. Some are people who live down the street from you. People from all walks of life speak out and act on their beliefs. Age is not a factor. People of all ages work to make the world a better place, including teenagers, young adults, middle-aged people, and the elderly.

What sets these people apart? They are aware of the needs of others. They have enthusiasm for improving things. And they feel a passion for a cause; it inspires them to try to make changes, to address issues, and to work to solve problems. Perhaps, in your heart, you are this kind of person—a person who acts on your beliefs.

People Who Make a Difference

Some individuals are very good at solving problems. Nothing is more rewarding to them than to try to solve a problem as soon as they see it. They don't care if the issue is complex or sensitive. Drawing on their energy and determination, these individuals search for solutions to injustice, intolerance, inequality, and people in need. They stand up for what they believe in and speak out to make the world a better place for everyone. Who are these people? In this section, you'll meet several.

You can use many types of resources to find evidence of people making the world a better place. You can look on the Internet, in encyclopedias, reference books, booklets from various agencies, magazines, and newspapers, to name a few.

Reading Hint

As you read the material on the following pages, think about what these individuals believe in and what problems they are trying to solve.

Students in Ms. Sneddon's class have strong feelings about how people treat one another. They regularly debate their views about issues that concern them. Sometimes they come up with ideas for making the world a better place. What issues concern you?

Netscape: Free The Children International

Back   Forward   Reload   Home   Search   Guide   Images   Print   Security   Stop

Location: http://www.freethechildren.com/

FREE THE CHILDREN

Information
Campaigns
Issues
Projects
Chapters
News & Media
Speakers Bureau
Get Involved
About Craig
Book and Video
L.E.A.D.
Donate
Search
Contact Us

Craig Kielburger is the 16 year old founder of *Free the Children*, an international children's ogranization in more than 20 countries, whose mission is to free children from poverty and exploitation and to empower young people to become leaders in their communities, nationally and internationally. Craig first became an advocate for children's rights when he was 12 years of age and read about the murder of a child from Pakistan sold into bondage as a carpet weaver.

In the past four years, Craig has traveled to more than 30 countries around the world visiting street and working children and speaking out in defence of children's rights. He is a much in demand speaker who has addressed students from primary to university levels, educatoros, government officials, business leaders and human rights gatherings on youth empowerement and the rights of children and young people.

Free the Children has initiated many projects all over the world, including the opening of schools and rehabilitation center for children, the creation of alternative sources of revenue for poor families to free children from hazardous work, leadership  programs for youth and projects linking children on an international level. Young people from *Free the Children* have helped to convince members of the business community to adopt codes of conduct in regards to child labor and governments to change laws to better protect children from sexual exploitation.

Craig has has gained international recognition from his appearances on CNN, 60 Minutes, and major television networks in North and South America and Europe. A documentary on his work won he 1999 Gold level UNESCO award at the New York Film Festival. His efforts on behalf of working, poor, and marginalized youth have been featured in major print media, including the New York Times, the Chicago Tribune, Newsweek, Stern, Point de Vue and the Times of London.

 Craig has reveived many awards for his work, including the State of the World Forum Award and the Roosevelt Freedom Medal (with Free the Children). He was named a Global Leader of Tomorrow at the World Economic Forum in Davos, Switzerland, and Ambassador of the First Children's Embassy in Sarajevo.

Craig's first book Free The Children was recently published by Harper Collins in the United States, McClelland and Stewart in Canada and Econ in Germany. It is currently being translated into French, Spanish and Chinese.

From the Free the Children Web site: http://www.freethechildren.com/ ,2000

When people **exploit** children, they use them to benefit themselves. An **advocate** for children is a person who speaks up for them.

Canadian Named To Prestige Posting

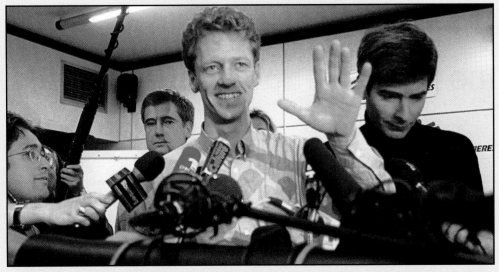

Dr. James Orbinski, president of Doctors Without Borders

By Richard Foot (Southam News)

In the desperate, menacing days of September 1992, when Somalia had collapsed into famine and anarchy [disorder], James Orbinski made a risky landing. The young Canadian doctor was flying in aboard a US Hercules relief flight, to take up a position with *Mèdecins Sans Frontiéres—Doctors Without Borders*—in the dusty, war-ridden town of Baidoa.

Orbinski had to jump from the rear cargo door as the airplane, under fire from warlord soldiers, made only a rolling stop on the airstrip before taking off again into the safety of the distant sky.

Minutes before Orbinski leaped into the Somali inferno [scene of horror], a crewmember on board turned to him and said, "I don't know why you people do this. But I'll tell you something, I'm sure glad somebody does." Like the US crew [member], most of us who stay at home like to see the flow of blood stopped and the empty stomachs filled, but who's willing to risk their life by getting off the airplane to make it happen?

Dr. James Orbinski is. The 38-year-old Canadian has saved countless lives in war zones and refugee camps around the world. Orbinski has returned to Canada from various hot zones malnourished, sick, and sometimes roughed up. He has done tours of duty in Cambodia, Somalia, Afghanistan, Rwanda, and the former Zaire. He has also worked with *Street Kids International* in Brazil.

Now he faces a new challenge as the first non-European president of the international council of *Doctors Without Borders*, one of the world's largest and most widely respected foreign aid organizations. The organization was formed in 1971 by a small group of French doctors who had helped victims of famine and war in Nigeria. Today *Doctors Without Borders* has blossomed into the largest deliverer of emergency medical care with 2000 volunteers working in 80 countries.

Dr. Orbinski hopes to use his term as the president of *Doctors Without Borders* to remind the world that helping others is not only an act of charity, but of duty. "People have a right to assistance in their times of crisis, and there is a duty on the part of the global human community to address that."

Excerpts from "Canadian named to prestige posting," *Vancouver Sun*, Sat., Aug. 22, 1998

Sometimes people take great personal risks as they make efforts to change the world in large and small ways.

Anti-personnel [ant-ee-pur-suh-NEL] **mines** are bombs in the ground. They are designed to blow up when a person steps on them.

Martin Luther King Jr., was famous for his work in fighting for civil rights. Videos are often a good source for biographies of famous people like him.

For Immediate Release
The Norwegian Nobel Institute
Drammensveien 19, N-0255 OSLO, Norway

The Nobel Peace Prize for 1997

International Campaign to Ban Landmines (ICBL)

The Norwegian Nobel Committee has decided to award the Nobel Peace Prize for 1997, in two equal parts, to the **International Campaign to Ban Landmines (ICBL)** and to the campaign's co-ordinator, **Jody Williams**, for their work for the banning and clearing of anti-personnel mines.

There are at present probably over one hundred million anti-personnel mines scattered over large areas on several continents. Such mines maim and kill indiscriminately and are a major threat to the civilian populations and to the social and economic development of the many countries affected.

The ICBL and Jody Williams started a process that in the space of a few years changed a ban on anti-personnel mines from a vision to a feasible reality. The Convention, which will be signed in Ottawa in December this year, is to a considerable extent a result of their important work.

There are already over 1000 organizations, large and small, affiliated to the ICBL, making up a network through which it has been possible to express and mediate a broad wave of popular commitment in an unprecedented way. With the governments of several small and medium-sized countries taking the issue up and taking steps to deal with it, this work has grown into a convincing example of an effective policy for peace.

The Norwegian Nobel Committee wishes to express the hope that the Ottawa process will win even wider support. As a model for similar processes in the future, it could prove of decisive importance to the international effort for disarmament and peace.

From The Norwegian Nobel Institute web site at http://www.nobel.no/97eng.html, 1997

Try This

On the previous three pages, you've read about the efforts of several people to improve the human condition. In a chart, summarize their efforts, using the following questions to get you started.

- What was the problem each was trying to solve?
- What change did each want to make?
- What did each do to make the change?
- What did each accomplish and how much remains to be done?

Investigate

In a group, brainstorm a list of people who have made a difference. Select one individual who has made a difference, and research his or her life and contributions. Describe an event at which this person made a difference. Ask yourself, "What problems did this person attempt to solve? What did he or she accomplish?"

Identify the personal characteristics that you think contributed to this person's successes. What characteristics do you think allowed this individual to be a leader?

Volunteering

Statistics show that one in three Canadian adults volunteer regularly. The value of all their work is over 16 billion dollars. This figure does not even include the contributions of the many teen and preteen volunteers in Canada. What other interesting facts can you see in the table below?

What makes these people do it? Why do they give freely of their time to help others? No one really knows for sure. One survey shows that teenagers who volunteer often end up volunteering for the rest of their lives.

For many young people, volunteering is a satisfying way to spend time. While helping others, you can meet new friends and learn new skills. Volunteering can also give you career ideas. And all volunteer work looks good on your résumé.

Volunteerism in Canada	
Total number of volunteers:	7 472 000
Participation rate of all Canadians:	31.4 per cent
Total hours volunteered:	1.11 billion
Economic value:	$16.3 billion
Number of full-time job equivalents:	578 000
Male to female ratio of volunteers:	46 to 54
Volunteers with jobs:	65 per cent
Province whose volunteers worked the most hours:	British Columbia (169 hours per year)
Province with the highest volunteer rate:	Saskatchewan (47 per cent)

"Volunteering"
by Happy Volunteer, age 13

I think that volunteering is a great way to help others. There are many people out there less fortunate than you are that you can help. It makes you and them happy. I volunteer at a geriatric home in my town. There are many elderly residents there. Most are over 87 years old. They have lived happy lives, but now they are so old that many of them have physical and mental problems. I know that they might not get better, so I am patient with them and help out the best I can. These seniors are wonderful people and I look forward to seeing them every time I go to the center. Volunteering is such a wonderful thing to do!! Call a shelter, home for special needs, or an event to raise charity money near to you and ask if you can volunteer to help out there.

A **geriatric home** is a nursing home for elderly people.

People volunteer for many different reasons. What motivated the "Happy Volunteer"?

Today, young people are volunteering more than ever. Businesses and non-profit groups are learning to make it known that they need help. If you did a search on the Internet, you would find many examples of teens volunteering at animal shelters, conducting recycling drives, reading to young children, helping at theatres, and spending time with senior citizens.

You Can Make a Difference

If you thought you could make a difference, would you be willing to try? Think about your community and the world. Do you see a problem that needs to be solved? Get together with a few other students, and choose a problem that interests all of you. To help you figure out how to solve it, read "How to Solve Problems."

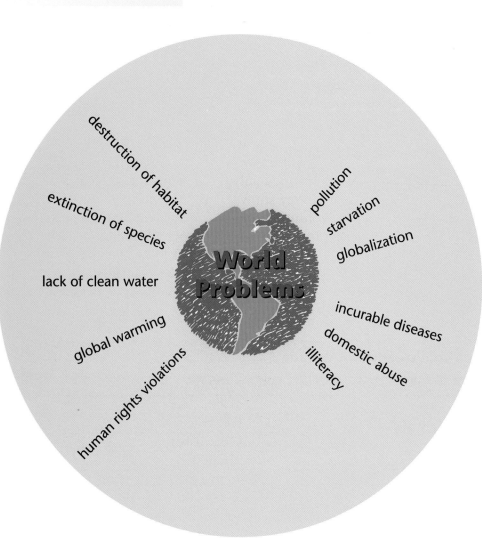

World Problems

destruction of habitat
extinction of species
lack of clean water
global warming
human rights violations
pollution
starvation
globalization
incurable diseases
domestic abuse
illiteracy

Many issues inspire people to action. Which of these inspires you?

HOW TO... Solve Problems

To find a solution to a problem, it helps to begin by asking yourself questions. Just jot down all the questions you have about the problem, its causes, and possible solutions.

The problem you want to solve may affect you alone or everyone in your community—or everyone on earth. In any case, you will find it helps to use some of the following strategies to find a way to make a difference.

1. First, figure out exactly what the problem is. Write down everything you know about the problem. Don't forget possible causes. If you need more information, get it.

2. Decide if you think you can tackle the whole problem, or if the problem is too big. Sometimes it makes more sense to solve one aspect of a problem. For example, world hunger might seem too big a problem. Hunger in a specific country might be easier to tackle.

3. To figure out what aspect of a problem you want to tackle, you'll have to decide which parts of the problem are most important. You also have to consider which parts you have the ability to influence. For example, you might have better luck protecting a Canadian endangered species rather than an Asian endangered species. It helps to write down your thoughts. Sometimes it helps to try to explain the problem to someone else.

What causes it?

Who's responsible?

How does it affect me?

Global Warming

What international agreements concern global warming?

How can we prevent it?

What harm does it do?

4. Think about what kind of solution you are trying to reach. This will give you a starting point to work back from. Break the problem into smaller pieces. If you start with the easiest parts first, you will usually be better prepared to take on the harder parts.

5. Think of similar problems you have dealt with in the past and how you solved them. For example, you might recall how your school solved a traffic problem by lobbying politicians to put in a crosswalk. Sometimes it helps to ask people how they solved similar problems or to read about how others have solved problems.

6. Figure out what you need to do or get before you can take action. It might be getting someone's help or co-operation, or it might be finding more information. Sometimes you will find that figuring out the cause of a problem will lead you to a solution.

Think For Yourself

1. You and a small group of classmates have been asked by the community council to solve a local problem of your choosing. You will need a desire to help others, some ideas about what your community needs, a goal to accomplish, and a plan that will make it happen.

   OR

2. You and a small group of classmates have been asked by the community to form a committee to address a global problem of your choosing. You are to present a plan and recommendations for action to the appropriate board of the United Nations. Design a course of action to solve the problem, including a set of recommendations for action.

To analyze your work on these activities, you can use the list of criteria given below.

When you develop plans to solve problems, you can use this list of criteria to check if you're on track.

Your plan shows that...

- You have clearly described the problem, issue, or inquiry.
- You have identified gaps in information needed to solve the problem or address the issue.
- You are aware of competing points of view or possible opposition to your proposed solution or course of action.
- You have included enough detail to put the plan into action.
- You have described the benefits of the course of action. That is, you have given logical reasons why the course of action should be followed.

Looking Back

In this book, you have seen that ancient civilizations and Canadian civilization share many features. In this chapter, you have seen that through the efforts of individual people we can make the world a better place. What kind of world do you want to live in? What can you do to help us get there?

Index

Numbers in boldface indicate an illustration

Acknowledgements

The author and publisher wish to thank Caren Cameron, Elementary Consultant (on leave) School District #62, Sooke, for her assistance in developing instructional strategies for students who will use this book.

The author and publisher also wish to thank the following consultants who provided guidance and advice:

Prof. Gordon Anderson,
Coordinator of East Asia Studies
Vanier College, York University

Sheila Borman
Principal of Kitchener Elementary
Burnaby, BC

Dr. Roland Case
Faculty of Education
Simon Fraser University

Al Mouner
Millstream Elementary School
School District #62, Sooke, BC

Dr. N.K. Wagle
Professor and Director,
Centre for South Asian Studies
University of Toronto

The author and publisher also extend their thanks to the following people for reviewing the manuscript:

Donna Anderson
Coal Tyee Elementary School
Nanaimo, BC

Wade Blake
Rutherford Community School
Nanaimo, BC

Sheila Borman
Kitchener Elementary School
Burnaby, BC

Mary Philpott
Hillside Elementary School
Mission, BC

Maureen Swoboda
Sidney, BC

Also thanks to the following people who helped in various ways during the development of the manuscript:

H. Saren S. Ghai,
namaste Canada

John Nadler
Journalist, Balkans

Ms April Snedden and her class at Royal Oak Middle School, especially Lynne Bezuidenhout, Chelsea Burns, Harrison Parker, and Warren Pratt School District #63, Saanich, BC

Dr. Hari M. Srivastava
University of Victoria

Credits

Cover Design: Brett Miller

Text Design: Paul Sneath/Brett Miller

Layout, Computer Graphics and Cartographic Art: Paul Sneath

Technical Art: VISU*TronX*, Paul Sneath

Illustrations: Nicolas Debon (36 – 37, 47 – 49, 51, 52, 54, 138, 155, 165, 178, 180, 188 – 89), Heather Graham (62 – 63, 73, 75, 92, 93, 98, 99, 135, 157, 187, 195), Caroline Price (42, 162 – 63), Michael Bowness (32, 205)

Cover Image: Glen Allison/Stone

Photo Credits

p. 1   CORBIS/AFP;

p. 15   CORBIS/AFP;

p. 17   CORBIS/Dave G. Houser;

p. 19   (left) CIDA/Brian Atkinson, (right) CIDA/David Trattles;

p. 23   Visuals Unlimited/A.J. Copley;

p. 27   J. Eastcott/Y. Momatuik/VALAN PHOTOS;

p. 28   (top) CORBIS/Arne Hodalic, (bottom) R. Burri/Magnum Photos;

p. 30   Cambridge University Collection;

p. 31   John Reader/Science Photo Library/Photo Researchers;

p. 33   Giraudon/Art Resource, NY;

p. 35   Sygma/Archives Innsbrook, Austria;

p. 40   Visuals Unlimited/Nada Pecnik;

p. 57   (left, right) CORBIS/Gunter Marx;

p. 58   Palestine Exploration Fund;

p. 60   Christine Osbourne/VALAN PHOTOS;

p. 61   Tony Stone/Richard Cooke III;

p. 66   CORBIS/Nik Wheeler;

p. 70   Canadian Press;

p. 76   CORBIS;

p. 77   (left, right) Erich Lessing/Art Resource;

p. 78   Erich Lessing/Art Resource;

p. 83   CORBIS/Gianni Dagli Orti;

p. 87   CORBIS/Digital Image © 1996 CORBIS;

p. 91   CORBIS/Gianni Dagli Orti;

p. 94   CORBIS/Roger Wood;

p. 102   CORBIS/Larry Lee;

p. 103   (left) CORBIS/Gianni Dagli Orti, (right) CORBIS/Ruggero Vanni;

p. 104   Tony Stone/Mike McQueen;

p. 109   CORBIS/Archivo Iconografico, S. A.

p. 110   CORBIS/Brian Vikander;

p. 114   CORBIS/Diego Lezama Orezzoli;

p. 115   (top) CORBIS/Archivo Iconografico, S. A., (bottom) CORBIS/Angelo Hornak;

p. 116   CORBIS/Charles & Josette Lenars;

p. 118   Woodfin Camp & Associates;

p. 119   Al Harvey/The Slide Farm;

p. 120   (left) CORBIS/Jeremy Horner, (right) CORBIS/Reuters Newmedia Inc.;

p. 121   (top left) CORBIS/Barnabas Bosshart, (bottom left) CORBIS/Brian Vikander, (top right) CORBIS/Peter Turnley, (bottom right) CORBIS/Nazima Kowall;

p. 122   CORBIS/Earl Kowall;

p. 123   CORBIS/Angelo Hornak;

p. 127   CORBIS/Jan Butchofsky-Houser;

p. 128   CORBIS/Brian Vikander;

p. 131   (left) Art Resource, NY, (right) CORBIS/Peter Turnley;

p. 132   NASA;

p. 133   CORBIS/Galen Rowell;

p. 136   CORBIS/Michael S. Yamashita;

p. 137   CORBIS/Royal Ontario Museum;

p. 140   CORBIS/Keren Su;

p. 142   CORBIS/Julia Waterlow; Eye Ubiquitous;

p. 143   CORBIS/Archivo Iconografico, S.A.;

p. 144   Al Harvey/The Slide Farm;

p. 145   CORBIS/David Samuel Robbins;

p. 148   CORBIS/Asian Art & Archaeology, Inc.;

p. 149   Granger Collection, NY;

p. 158   CORBIS/Underwood & Underwood;

p. 160   Granger Collection, NY;

p. 161   CORBIS/Reuters Newmedia Inc.;

p. 169   (top) CORBIS/Dallas and John Heaton, (bottom) CORBIS/Michael Nicholson;

p. 175   CORBIS/Adam Wolfitt;

p. 182   CORBIS/Araldo de Luca;

p. 183   CORBIS/Jeremy Horner;

p. 184   (top) CORBIS/Archivo Iconografico, S.A., (middle) CORBIS/Vanni Archive, (bottom) Margaret Hoogeveen;

p. 191   Men in chains and a circus scene, three register relief, 3rd century AD (marble) Ashmolean Museum, Oxford, UK/Bridgeman Art Library

p. 192   (left) CORBIS/Dave Bartruff, (right) Art Resource, NY;

p. 194   Canadian Press/Jacques Boissinot;

p. 198   (top) Granger Collection, NY, (middle) CORBIS/AFP;

p. 200   Canadian Press;

p. 202   Canadian Press/Jacques Boissinot;

p. 203   Canadian Press/Chuck Stoody;

p. 209   AP/Wide World Photos Inc./Remy de la Mauviniere

Text Credits

pp. 41 – 42   'The Maya' abridged from *Human Antiquity: An Introduction to Physical Anthropology and Archaeology*, Second Edition, by Kenneth L. Feder and Michael A. Park. Copyright © 1992 by Mayfield Publishing Company. Reprinted by permission of the publisher;

pp. 56 – 57   Excerpted and adapted from 'The Development of Farming' from *Man's Place in Evolution* (London: The Natural History Museum, 1991), pp. 86 – 91. © The Natural History Museum, London. Reprinted by permission;

pp. 74 – 75   Excerpts from 'A Stranger in Nippur' from *The Sumerians: Inventors and Builders* by Elizabeth Lansing (New York: McGraw-Hill Books Company, 1971), pp. 54 – 61. Reprinted by permission of The McGraw-Hill Companies;

p. 137   'Return Home' by Tao Yuanming from *Great Literature of the Eastern World* edited by Ian P. McGreal. Copyright © 1996 by Ian P. McGreal. Reprinted by permission of HarperCollins Publishers, Inc.;

p. 166   MacKendrick, Paul L., *Classics in Translation*, Volume 1. © 1952. Reprinted by permission of The University of Wisconsin Press.;

p. 179 – 81   Excerpts from *Song for a Dark Queen* by Rosemary Sutcliff (London: Pelham Books, 1978). Reprinted by permission of David Higham Associates;

p. 208   The Free the Children web site: http://www.freethechildren.com/, 2000. Reprinted by permission.

p. 209   Richard Foot (Southam News), excerpts from 'Canadian named to prestige posting' from *The Vancouver Sun*, 22 August 1998;

p. 210   Copyright © The Nobel Foundation, Stockholm, 1997;

p. 211   Table from Silverplatter International N.V., http://erl.micromedia.on.ca, 1996

p. 212   "Volunteering" by Happy Volunteer, age 13, from http://www.zuzu.org. Reprinted by permission.

Every effort has been made to trace the original source of material and photographs contained in this book. Where the attempt has been unsuccessful, the publisher would be pleased to hear from copyright holders to rectify any omissions.

Ancient Worlds Featured in This Text

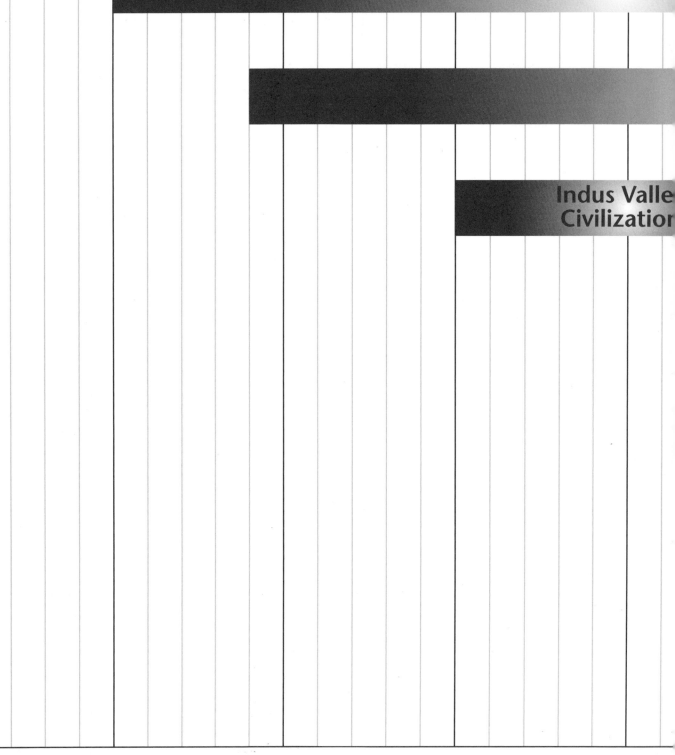

Mesopotamia

Indus Valley
Civilization

4000 BCE   3500   3000   2500 BCE   2000